Dark Inheritance

A BILLIONAIRE BOSS ROMANCE

REBECCA BAKER

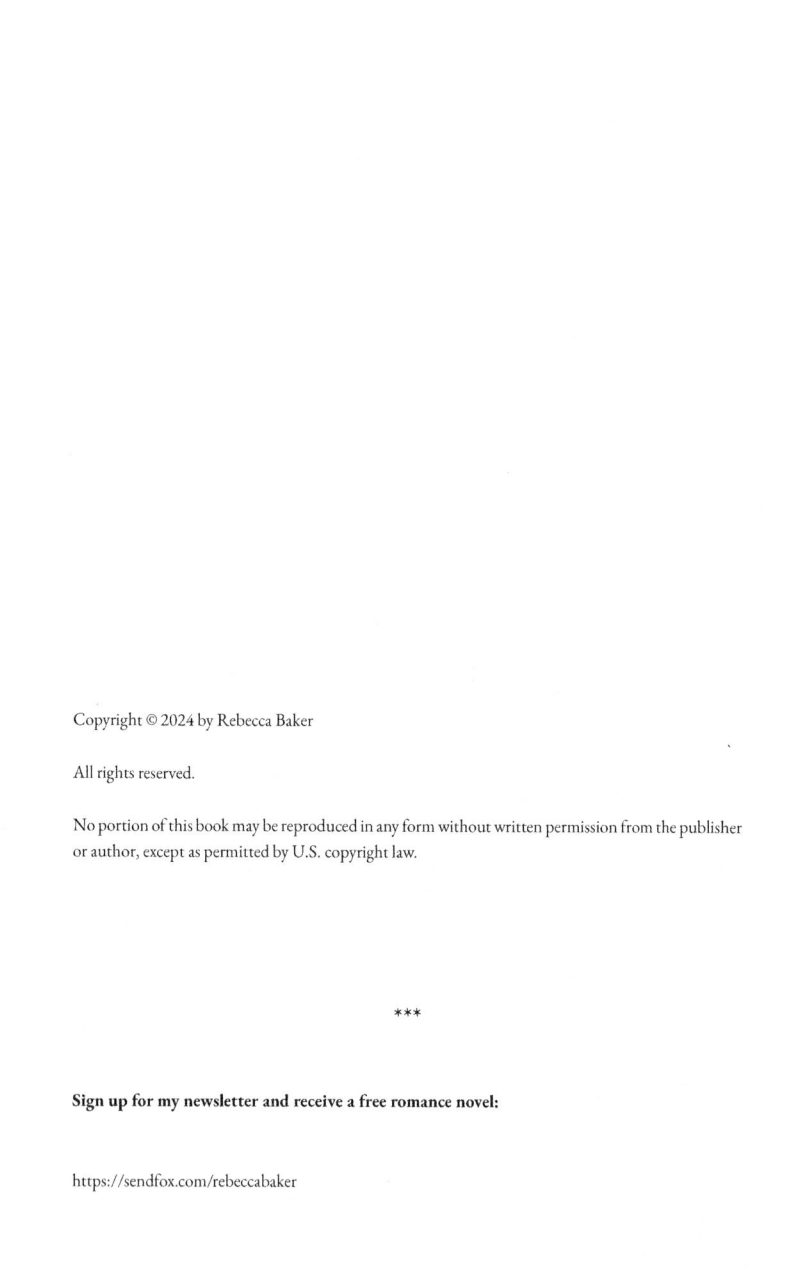

Copyright © 2024 by Rebecca Baker

All rights reserved.

No portion of this book may be reproduced in any form without written permission from the publisher or author, except as permitted by U.S. copyright law.

***

Sign up for my newsletter and receive a free romance novel:

https://sendfox.com/rebeccabaker

Chapter One

HUDSON

Sinclair.

My last name is synonymous with power, exclusivity, and money.

Everyone knows that. The name means billions. Respect. Quality. And with it, I've anyone I want, everything I want.

Except maybe this...

If it's true, that is.

I stare down at the letter long after my father's lawyer leaves.

A small thrill, like smoke, twists through me.

Fuck. The Sinclair jewels, things of myth and legend. They might be true.

If I'm to believe the letter and my father's lawyer.

It's the one-year anniversary of his death, and he was a hard man to love. Respect, yes. Love... no. But it isn't about love, no matter what people say. Respect, integrity, work, power, those are the things that matter.

So this letter, the visit, and everything with it are all completely unexpected.

I run my thumb over the envelope.

The paper is thick, handmade, top of the game in its craftsmanship. That was my old man all over. Every single detail to him mattered, and it seems, still does.

Even long after his death.

Hudson Sinclair. My name's written on the front in strong penmanship. A dark brown-black ink. Fountain pen. Old with a gold nib from the shading and line thickness differences.

Pity my father hadn't cared about people as much as he did about things and money and the Sinclair empire.

Then again, would my brothers and I be here if he hadn't? Maybe. Maybe not. We'd be somewhere in the top percentile, I know that. We were all born with the need for power and money and success.

But this...

It brings everything into a different playing field. Not that I have much time for play.

I sit back in the leather chair in my office. It's late, after nine in the evening, but the office of my own empire still ticks. I work hard and I expect my staff to do the same.

For once, my mind isn't on work.

Without another thought, I send a group text to my brothers.

That little thrill inside grows, fans its own flames.

Making money comes easy. Hard work beats like the blood in my veins. But this, oh fuck yeah, this is my heritage, my legacy, an unexpected inheritance, and the one thing money can't buy.

And the more I think about it, the more I want.

The phone pings with responses and for once my siblings are within a five-block radius so it shouldn't be long. I'd put it down to kismet or some such bullshit if I actually believed.

In the meantime, I need to make some calls...

Ten minutes later, my brother, Ryder, pushes open my office door and sticks his dark head into my office, all without bothering to knock.

"Hey, man," he says, sauntering in, "what's the big deal? I got a date. Two actually. Couldn't decide which lucky lady gets me."

"Now there's a shocker." I tap the envelope on my antique desk. "Only two?"

"It's Monday. I've got a long week. You should see the blonde, legs right up to here." He places a hand somewhere around his head. "And the redhead, she's—"

"This better be good." Magnus, one of my other brothers, comes in after a sharp, hard rap, followed by Kingston, who already looks bored out of his brain. He's checked his watch about five times since he arrived a second ago.

I know the feeling. I'm busy, too.

We all are.

We might be heirs to a multibillion dollar real estate empire known across the planet, but we've made our own fortunes, too. Made our own billions. Our father believed in giving us money in our pockets, an education, and letting us make our own way.

It wasn't like the old man let us do what we wanted. He pushed. He played hardball and drove ethics—his version—into us. Not even our mother, when they were married, could get him to go easy.

But his style made us the best of the best and I don't think we'd be anything else than what we are. Apart from his push, the Sinclair drive is in our blood. Money and success come first. Always.

Even at the top of our games, we have our own goals in our own businesses, and are name only in the Sinclair flagship, but we push on. There's nothing but more money, more respect, more power to have.

Except, perhaps, this.

The contents of my letter.

I motion for them all to sit. I've exactly half an hour before I have to get back to work. I'd been hoping to fuck the sexy socialite who'd been chasing me hard for the past few weeks. She's gorgeous, hot, and a way to get off. But this is eating into my time, so no socialite for me. Not tonight, anyway.

And this is more important than run-of-the-mill sex.

"The Sinclair jewels," I say. "They exist."

"The legendary family jewels?" Ryder, the ass, starts laughing, stretching out on the black leather armchair in the area where I hold informal meetings. "They don't." Then he stops. "Do they?"

"Apparently." I rise from behind my desk and pull the letter from the envelope and smooth it open.

Ryder reaches up and snatches it from me, letting out a low whistle as he scans it. "Well."

Magnus stalks over from where he stands in his dark gray three-piece suit and takes the letter. Then he tosses it on the hand cut rust-colored marble coffee table. "We don't need the money."

"Gimmick." Kingston crosses the office and reads it as it lays there. Then he shoves his hands in the pockets of his jeans.

"According to this, there are four jewels. We all thought they were lost, or a story. But according to Jenson, and this letter, they're very real."

"We don't need a story according to father's lawyer, and we don't need the family jewels," Kingston says, glancing at us all. "We're rich enough."

"It's not just the jewels," I shoot back, smoothing a hand down my waistcoat as I think about my next words. "They were important to our father, and since they're real and this is a way to get my hands on one, I'm not letting it pass. This is a piece of our family dynasty. A part of what it means to be a Sinclair. People have coveted these jewels for decades. They're talked about, and—"

"Jesus, Hudson." Magnus lifts a brow. "People also think they're residing in some secret private show room with half the art that's been stolen or rumored to have been stolen over the years. People are people and they piss me the fuck off. I don't need to join in on a rumor."

"No, but this is from our father."

"Dear old Dad," says Ryder, swinging one leg over the other as he gets comfortable, "the man with a plan even from beyond the grave."

"You're a dick," mutters Kingston. "And I've got better things to do here. Okay, so they're real, and what? Did you read that thing?"

"Yes. And I listened to Jenson."

Magnus' mouth curves into a cynical smile. "It's a lot. And you don't have time for anything but work and some good old fashioned stress release."

Pot talking smack to the kettle, right there. I cross my arms. "It's not like I have to give up sex or cut into work."

"Okay, let's say this manipulation is worth it. What about us?"

"Maybe your own letter's waiting, Ry," I say.

"Maybe I don't want one."

But I know that's a lie. Ryder loves beautiful things. Rare things. Coveted things. And he'd always talked about the Sinclair jewels as a kid and teen, before sex and money really got in the way.

"Maybe you won't get a chance," Kingston says, and he ignores the dark look from Ryder. "Maybe it's just you. This sounds complicated. If they're there, we can contest—"

"I'll be having my lawyer look things over, but Jenson said it's airtight." And I have to sign a contract. I have four weeks once I do that to pull this off, to convince Jenson it is all legit, and then I can have my piece of the dynasty. Something that I can't buy and don't already have.

My brothers look at me and I straighten up. "I'm going to do it."

"You are?" Ryder frowns, glancing about.

"I said so, didn't I? It seems simple. Find a bride and convince the world I'm in love. Or Jenson, in this case. I'll put in some calls." I shoot a look at Magnus. "And don't judge. I'm not an idiot. It's not going to be real and no one will get hurt. A contract in a contract. This one very private, and with a woman who needs the money."

Kingston shakes his head. "That's stupid."

"It's trouble," says Ryder, "and I know trouble. Very well."

"Not if I do it right. I already put in some calls. A favor for a favor, and I already got a bite."

"Hud, you're never reckless, so why now?"

I cut a glare at Magnus. "I'm not. I'm streamlining. I've an old college buddy...they're a respected family, old money, and the kind of old money where it's name over cash and since the coffers are low, he said his cousin works for XO Temps, and is in need of more than her job pays." I pause, choosing my words carefully because I didn't exactly tell Bixby or anyone else what this was about, other than a demanding job that's going to pay well, as it's last minute.

I could have told him everything, and he'd only have heard money and a way to not spend his own. "Thinks she'd be willing to do it and...she's coming here tonight. I can give her a job and have it work that way."

"A cliché office romance?" Ryder asks. "It suits you."

"Thanks. How kind, asshole."

"I try."

Magnus starts laughing and shakes his head. "Better you than me, man. You haven't met her and you're gonna do this?"

"Yes," I say. "As long as she fits my criteria of honesty, and the ability to keep a secret, then it's good. And someone rich needing money means she's going to keep the damn secret." I start really warming to the idea. "She's not going to want more, and she'll know how to move in my world. And if she's already working, she's got integrity. As long as she has skill, I can hire her and that sets the stage."

"You know what happens on stages?" Ryder pipes up, setting both feet on the floor and standing. "Tragedies. Operas, farces. All of those have the kind of plots where things go very, very wrong."

"In your world, maybe, but not in mine. I'm not planning to fuck her, just marry her, pay her and send her on her way when we succeed. That's all."

Ryder sighs. "Boring. That's boring."

"That," I shoot back, "is streamline and success."

"Can I sleep with her?"

"No," I snap. "That's a complication, Ryder. And maybe she won't want to sleep with you."

He starts laughing like I've told the biggest joke in the world. "They all want to sleep with me."

My brother's a pretty boy and feckless. If he wasn't so damn smart and ruthless under all that charm, I'd be royally pissed off.

"There's always a first time," mutters Magnus.

"Or," chimes in Kingston, who doesn't seem quite so bored, "a third or a fourth."

"Lies." Ryder rubs his hands together. "When does she arrive?"

"About a minute after you all leave," I say.

"You invited us to leave?" Magnus gets that bullish expression on his chiseled face I know too well. "We might as well see her."

"I don't want to scare her immediately," I say. "I only wanted to give you all a heads up on what might be coming your way."

"Did you...tell her?" Ryder smirks.

I haven't even spoken to her, so I keep that to myself. "Out."

Kingston checks his watch. "I need to go, anyway. Let's leave him to fuck up his life."

And with that, he ushers the others out of the office, leaving me alone.

Fuck it up? Hardly. And it's four weeks.

If she doesn't fit what I want, then I'll find someone else. Quickly. But a rich girl with money problems? It seems perfect. And like I said, this is simple, an easy fix to get what I want.

What can possibly go wrong?

Right at that moment, a knock sounds at the door. I cross the office and pull it open, and suddenly I'm face to face with the woman who just might help me pull this off.

Chapter Two

SCARLETT

"I'm here."

Okay, I don't mean to do it. Honestly.

We-ell, sorta honestly.

But I'm at the door, face to face with the man who runs high-end real estate. An honest to goodness Sinclair billionaire of the Sinclair real estate empire fame—not that I care, but my brother does—and he's utterly damp in the panties and fluttery tummy gorgeous. This man can make pulses leap at more than ten paces.

I've overheard the conversation with his brothers. Just the tail end, but enough to know he's not just looking for someone to hire, but for a pretend fiancée. And I've just led him to believe it's me.

"Right on time," he says, in a voice like dark velvet that curls toes and makes heating obsolete. "Come in."

I clutch the padded envelope to me and follow him into the castle version of an office. It's gorgeous, but not like him.

He's tall, lean and can wear a suit like he's stepped off Tom Ford's runway. I'm not sure if Tom Ford has a bespoke runway, but if he did, this man would be the number one star. It's probably not even a Tom Ford suit. It'll be custom made because that's what it looks like, something crafted by hand and costing more money than I've ever seen in my lifetime.

I'm meant to just be couriering him the package, which is from XO Temps, courtesy of Sarah.

"So you know the deal?" he asks.

"Yes." I got the Cliff Notes version, but I'm good at outside the box thinking. I'd have to be, since artificial intelligence is my passion and training AIs is something I want to earn my living at.

Just as soon as I sort everything else out.

Which brings me back to this. The whole not meaning to do it.

He's looking at me. Dark gray eyes like a sky before a storm are on me and they're full of fire and intelligence and his mouth would be sensual if he didn't look so no-nonsense and grim. He raises a brow. Hudson, that's what Sarah called him. Her cousin's old college friend.

I'd planned just to hand the file to his receptionist, a harried woman in her fifties who looked like she wanted to be anywhere but here...but somehow the words I'm here to see Hudson Sinclair came from my mouth.

See? Not my fault.

"I'm Scarlett," I say, aiming for an approximation of charm and wishing I wasn't wearing spandex and an oversize shirt.

He frowns. "I thought Bixby said your name was Sarah..."

"Scarlett's what I go by."

"I may have misheard." It's the kind of tone that says he knows he didn't, but he's letting it slide. For now. "Bix and I aren't close, I'm afraid."

"Us either." Which is true as I've never met him. "It's a four-week gig, working for you and...I'm sorry, I just overheard it might be more than that."

He's nodding, and he crosses the room to lean on his desk as he takes me in. "You don't look like I expected."

I pop a hand on my hip and strike a Vogue pose. When he doesn't laugh, I bite down on a sigh and drop my hand. "I took up riding my bike. I was heading home when I got the call."

This is partly true. I ride because one of my gigs is couriering. And I happened to be there at XO after my final job finished because Sarah Merriweather is actually a friend. She comes from old money but never has it and burns through it like it's kindling.

Sarah's flighty. She's blond and pretty and fits the image he's got in his head of an heiress without the cash and a whole lot of need.

We had drinks planned, which always meant waiting forever for Sarah to get her shit together. And in the minutes between agreeing to meet Hudson Sinclair and solve all her immediate money needs with a stupidly well-paying job, she'd gotten a call from her man of the hour.

A rich oligarch who wooed her with the South of France.

No work in sight except to keep the guy happy.

So, in a panic, she'd thrown together a small list of potential replacements—who keeps dossiers on other people when you're not a spy?—and begged me to deliver them.

So here I am, not meaning to, but pretending to be my friend.

It won't hurt. It's all hush-hush and secretive. He wants something. I want something. Needs will be met and it's all just a contractual obligation. Still. I hold out the package.

He looks at it like I'm offering him dime store candy. With suspicion. "What is that?"

"I came prepared. Just in case you want someone else. Here's a selection." I pause, looking at the padded envelope. Down on his fancy floor are my sneakered feet. They're not even the good ones. The sneakers, I mean. I have the same feet I've always had. It's a thing. I've learned to live with it.

"You came here with other women in mind, in case I found you lacking?" he says in the exact voice people use for the potentially violent and unhinged. "For what you thought was a job?"

I nod. "And for a finder's fee."

"Of course." He frowned. "This isn't a joke, Scarlett."

"I know that."

"You were eavesdropping."

I shrug. "I overheard, that's all."

"That's all?" he asks. "All? It's my *life*."

I swallow, fingers biting into the soft cardboard and padding. "I know." No one knows Sarah's taken off. She's not close to her family, and I'm imagining her cousin who lives on the other side of the country figured this was an easy way to help her. "I don't usually look like this. Then again, I also work at a temp agency."

"Doing what?"

"PA." I say this as nonchalantly as I can. I've never done anything like that before. But does it matter? This is to convince a stuffy lawyer I'm in love and going to marry this man, which doesn't involve office work. I'm in lust with him on a superficial level already, so that will help.

I don't want to sleep with him. But admire him? Yep, I can do that. A lot. Maybe even for hours.

"What did you overhear?"

"You need a fiancée in four weeks. I don't know anything else except it's important and you're paying well."

"And you're okay with that?"

"You're paying well. Why wouldn't I be? As long as it's above board."

He frowns. "Obviously."

"You..." I take a breath. "You don't want to see the other women?"

"Fuck no. The fewer people who know about this the better. There'll be an NDA and contract, of course. With some added..." His gaze slides over me, "rules."

"I'm fine with that. I don't usually dress like this. As I said, I'm riding and I can't do that in a dress and heels."

I realize right then that I want this. Not just the job I thought was on offer for four weeks, but all of it. I wouldn't have jumped in by accident if I didn't, but I'm surprised with the slam of need and determination that hits me in this very second.

A four-week contract with Hudson Sinclair will get my brother out of the fix he's in, and I'll be able to more than make rent. Sarah didn't tell me the exact amount, but her vague hundreds of thousands she said he'll pay because he's in a bind is a godsend. Now I know what the bind is, at least surface-wise, I can do it. After all, it's just pretend. How hard can this be?

Not very is the only answer I can come up with.

"Is that a yes?" I ask.

"I'm not sure," he murmurs, crushing all my dreams of the moment. "Honestly, I wouldn't date you."

I narrow my eyes, toss the envelope down, and stalk up to him, poking him in the chest. Warmth zings through me at the contact. "That is rude."

"Scarlett." Up close I can smell him. Leather with a hint of lavender and dark honey that shouldn't work but does, and he closes a hand around mine, pulling it from his chest. I shiver, a thrum running through me of something that's suspiciously like wanting. "I just meant people who know me know the kind of woman I—date."

"You mean sleep with."

He ignores me. "I need someone who can keep up socially, and by that I mean look the part. I don't waste my time, so—"

"Have you heard of opposites attract?"

"I've heard of fairies in the bottom of the garden, but I don't believe in that either. I don't waste my time."

"You must be fun at parties."

He smiles and my knees turn wobbly and liquid. "I don't go to those kinds of parties."

"There are the other women here—"

"I said no to that." He tilts his head, looking at me, then shakes it. "If not you, I'll go back to the drawing board."

"I need this." The words are out before I can stop them. But something changes in his dark gray eyes, like a flash of heat lightning.

"The job part? That's real. You'd have to work for me, too."

"I assumed that." Inside, my mind won't stop yelling the word shit at me. "And with the rest? I'm very adaptable. But I can do the job in my sleep."

That's a total lie. But again, how hard can it be?

"That's another issue. I wouldn't hire you. You're in…shiny pants."

"Leggings." He's still holding my hand and his thumb is absently sliding over my knuckles, making me shiver with a thousand softly electrified nerve endings. And then I remember my bag. "Do you have an en suite?"

"Over there." He lets go of me and points to his left.

"One minute."

I turn, glad for the messenger bag strapped over my back, like a backward baby sling, and hurry into the restroom and close the door.

For a moment, I stop and turn in a circle.

Soft, recessed lighting, smooth cream stones and brass fixtures, complete with a flower arrangement that no doubt costs my monthly rent for my share of the ratty apartment that might once have been a shoebox, and dark olive green velvet seat.

It's got the usual. I say usual, because I'm sure most billionaires have a steam shower and bidet and two sinks. And what looks like a walk-in closet—okay, it is a walk-in closet because I cross and open the opaque door that leads through to a changing room and a view to drool over.

I don't for this. I stop and stare at myself in the floor-length mirror. Definitely don't have time. My hair's shoved in a mousey mess on my head and made worse by my helmet and the outfit...well, the less thought about that the better.

But, lucky for me, I have a change in my bag and I get down to business; peeling off leggings and socks and sneakers in one swoop, and then I follow with the T-shirt and hoodie.

I pull out the no-crease upscale looking trousers and fitted top, all in black, and shove my feet into low-heeled shoes. Then I pull down my hair and finger fluff.

There's no makeup in my bag except a tube of lipstick, so I apply that, and thank the powers that be I came prepared for drinks and upscale, even waitress outfits are so versatile.

I'm done and it took no more than five minutes.

Shoving everything in my bag, I hold it in one hand and return to the vast swanky office.

Hudson Sinclair looks up from where he's in the middle of texting on his phone and goes still. His gaze moves from the top of my head down to my shoes.

"Listen," I say, "I usually dress better than this, too. But I'm smart, I'm a hard worker, and you need help and I need money. This works. It makes sense. And, I'm here."

It occurs to me that's what he wants—excellence, no time wasted and ease. He's that kind of guy.

"And how hard can this be? Office romance?"

"Yes," he says. "That's what I was thinking."

"Pretend office romance," I add.

His expression says he wouldn't have it any other way, and I'm both insulted and relieved.

"Do I pass?"

"You know what?"

I close my eyes, knowing I've blown it. "What?"

"Let's go for it."

Inside, I do a fist pump. Outside, I open my eyes and smile the way I've seen Sarah smile at men. Not the I'm going to fuck you smile, but the demure, slightly pleased one. And that's about all I have when it comes to pretending to be her. She's little, I'm a lot taller. She's blonde, I'm saddled with light brown hair.

But he said yes, so I'm in.

"Where do we go from here, Mr. Sinclair?"

"Hudson," he says, holding out his hand. I put mine in his. "It's a deal, Scarlett Merriweather."

"Colton."

He frowns at me and I smile, gliding over the truth. "Cousins on mother's side to old Bix."

Hudson nods and I ignore the heat streaking through me at our clasped fingers.

"And as for where do we go from here? Success." He doesn't smile as he says this. "We make it work."

"I can do that."

"And, Scarlett? Don't betray or lie to me, or I'll destroy you."

Chapter Three

HUDSON

Scarlett Meriweather—Colton—is not what I expected.

I'm tempted to say she's from the poorer side of the Meriweather clan, except Bixby wouldn't bother with what he calls commoners. Even if they're family. Especially if they're family. Besides, his mother's family is Mayflower stock and blood so blue they probably can't spell poor. Scarlett might be the quirky one. Who knows? I don't, and I don't care, as long as she can do it.

And she doesn't come across as flighty. Which is a plus. Even if she's on the mouthy side. And probably hungry for more when it comes down to the dollar.

Still, Scarlett's like a breath of fresh air. One I'm not sure I want, but I've got.

For a moment, I wonder if I'm being a complete fucking moron. But it's too late for that. The idea is in my head, I've got the bull by the horns, and I'm not about to let go.

I want this.

I want what's mine, and this woman is the one who's going to help me achieve that.

I look her over again, and since now she's changed, I can definitely see our fake whirlwind relationship and engagement working.

Sure, I'm more than aware I'm cheating the system my father put in place, but he taught each and every one of us that only losers take the hardest path by rote. Instead, he was about finding ways around things, working smarter, being devious.

That's not about screwing people over. It's about finding the best way, and sometimes the best way is the hardest. Other times, it's finding the hidden door and for me, this is it.

I've no intention of finding a bride for real, as I know my father. The four weeks mean from now.

It might be worded in a way where I might be fooled into thinking there's a way to push it back, and I'm going to play hardball in checking that out, but the four weeks are four weeks and if Jenson turns up in three weeks, I'll guarantee the official documentation will have today's date on it.

But I've got Scarlett.

A secret weapon.

She's a little rough edged, but that might work in my favor. I'm no Pygmalion, but I don't want to be. I just want someone who might fit in, and a little unexpected will work.

Listening in at the door and working it all out shows smarts and initiative, which I like. And she's easy on the eye.

"I'm not a horse." She narrows her eyes a little.

My mouth twitches. "I didn't think you were."

"You're looking at me like one."

"A thoroughbred."

She presses her lips together and folds her hands in front of her. She's got a lithe body with a delightful swell of slender hips and small but perfect tits. Normally, I like something a little more...visual as I'm not planning on deep conversation or follow-ups unless the sex proves sensational. And even those encounters wane after the fourth or fifth time. Maybe if I was looking for a relationship I'd be interested in taking things further, but then again, apart from me not wanting that, I wouldn't pick the women I do.

They're sexy under a layer of class, but most of them I'm not interested in talking to. I don't have the time.

Scarlett's definitely not like anything I've seen. She doesn't have the air of entitlement like her brother. And she doesn't come across a snob or a name dropper or spoiled. I mean, she rides a damn bike in Manhattan for crying out loud. And not a Citi Bike from the outfit she wore, either. She owns the bike.

"Well," she says, with a nervous laugh, "what do we do now?" She looked at me, an uncertain light in her hazel eyes.

The combination of dark honey hair and warm eyes are a killer, and she has a mouth made for kissing.

"Unless you want to get right to the destruction of me," she adds.

I probably took things a bit far with the ultimation. I meant every word. But I could have softened it. Just a little.

"If you pull this off and don't lie to me, then I won't have to." I can still feel the heat of her fingers, the soft silk of her skin as I held her hand, something I didn't mean to do. The attraction is there, unexpected, a small flare of light I can use in this.

Because I want to win.

The letter only mentioned the jewels, but there's more, and I'll tell my brothers later. Right now, I need to get our ground rules down between me and Scarlett.

I motion to the leather sofa and she perches on it, while I take the seat next to her, crossing my legs as she tucks her feet below her on the floor, her knees pressed together. "I wish I could say I didn't mean to come on strong, but that's not true. I don't do things like this and I'm private. I'm not on page six or whichever damn page it is, and I want to keep it that way. So if you're into getting your five minutes, this won't work."

"I'm not going to Warhol you. Although in that case, it would be fifteen minutes." She stops, pink blooming in her cheeks. "I'm good with that."

"Good, because this is my reputation on the line, and I don't screw things up. I make level headed, intelligent decisions, so don't make me regret this one."

"I got that with the retribution thing."

I laugh, unable to help myself. Even though the situation isn't funny, she is. She has a self-deprecating streak that's likable.

Thing is, I don't need to like her. I need her to make this happen for me.

The jewels, or jewel that's got my name on it, isn't the only thing up for grabs according to Jenson. It's a slice of the pie. A stake—a real one—in the family company. We all have shares but we have no power and that's how dear old Dad set it up. That's been fine, but to have a piece of my namesake in the form of a real say, and if I'm reading Jenson right, it will keep the balance private and not public. And that means Sinclair, the flagship company, remains in family hands...or the board of directors. But if I fail, then more shares will be sold and that could tip things into the public realm.

It's a pride thing, and I'm probably making more of it than I need to. But these are some of the shares held in my father's name and they go to me or to be sold to the public, and I don't want that. At all.

"It's a big job, which is why I'm not only paying well, along with the payout. I gave your brother a ballpark figure, told him I needed someone to fill a particular role. That's it. And I'm going to expect you to do that job."

Her eyes go big and the pink turns red in her cheeks.

I smooth a hand down along my thigh. Christ, you'd think I'm asking her to fuck me. Business is business, and this is business. I don't ever mix that with pleasure.

"That job is as my assistant. And I'm officially hiring you. So you'll need to do it well. If you're good enough, we'll talk about continuing the job when the engagement contract is fulfilled."

"Okay." She leans in a little and the subtle scent of flowers teases my senses. Not sweet, but fresh, just picked, with an earthiness to it, a greenness that's refreshing. "You get the bonus of help and we can use it to speed this up in a natural seeming way."

"Exactly."

It sounds like we're discussing the driest of dry business deals. Which, I guess we are.

But it has to be this way. Four weeks might seem like nothing, but they could change everything. And I want that change in my favor. Completely.

"I guess we should get to know each other? Or wait until you have a contract—"

"I'll have that stuff for you bright and early tomorrow." I let my gaze slide over her again, lingering a little too long on that soft looking mouth of hers.

When I realize what I'm doing, I drag my eyes away and check my Rolex. It used to be my grandfather's on my mother's side. I have work to do, both in my own business and with this.

"You can sign that contract and NDA and then—"

"In four weeks, we part ways."

"I need you to work starting tomorrow. It'll be light, a day to settle in. I'm fair, but I expect..." I try to think of the right word when she speaks.

"Blood?"

"More or less." I shoot her an assessing look. "Nervous?"

"No."

I smile and stand. "In four weeks we're going to have to convince those who matter that we're in love. And the moment the dotted line is signed between us, we'll get down into that."

"Blood, guts, hard work, whirlwind fake romance. I'm hoping there's a Hallmark card I can get you at the end of this."

She's definitely an unexpected breath of fresh air and she can make me smile, even laugh. I think I'm going to enjoy getting to know her. But... "Scarlett, this thing, it really does depend on total honesty."

Scarlett glances at her hands and takes a breath, and then she looks at at me. "Of course. I don't want this out there, either."

"People will know of the engagement when it happens, and then we'll let things end when I say so." I sit down again, a nervous energy whispering in my veins and I cross my legs once more. "A fight? I'll think of something."

She nods. "We can do this." And then she leans over and places her hand on mine. Awareness shoots through me, right down to my cock, and I'm thankful I've got my legs crossed. "So, do we swap birthdays, all of that?"

"Just getting to know each other to start is good." If I know Jenson, he'll be looking for that ease, that familiarity. "Everything else will come."

She blows out a breath and laughs. "This is going to be interesting." Then she looks down, and I can see the moment the realization hits her that she's got her hand on mine and she's suddenly a deer in headlights for a second before she pulls away.

"And the honesty," I say.

"Honesty." She flashes a smile that hits hard. It's a mix of minx and sweetness and nerves all bundled together and it's intoxicating.

I'm hungry, that's all. I missed my dinner meeting, and in the back of my head I'm doing mental Tetris with all the other things I need to get done. Dinner is now meant to be late night drinks that I'm going to have to make happen as it's an important business meet. But I want—need—to spend time with Scarlett.

"When do we get started?" she asks brightly. "In the morning?"

"Hell no," I say. "We start now."

Chapter Four

SCARLETT

Ooookay, so I might have bitten off a little bit more than I can chew. The whole eyes too big for the stomach metaphor. But...and there's a but, I decide as I hug my old ratty bear, Mr. Figglesmort to me as I stare up at the ceiling that night.

Hudson is a tall, gorgeous drink of...not water. I'm going with something unexpected, like a dry vodka martini with a hint of olive juice and herb twist. Something with a little spice and flavor you think is just gloriously mixed to taste like water and then it hits you.

I squeeze my eyes shut.

I'm all over the place with these analogies, but it's not like I go around leaping into someone else's shoes and pretending to fall in love. It's stupid. It's...surreal.

We spent about forty minutes in his office chatting about this and that. Movies and food and drinks. He likes fine dining and the fanciest place I've been was an Italian joint with red tablecloths and candles on the Upper West Side a few years back when some guy was trying to impress me right out of my panties and onto his dick. It didn't work. I got food poisoning and I wasn't into him.

That's not the point.

The point is, I stuck as close to the truth without giving it. Sarah's been all over the place, to the trendiest spots in town. When you have the right name, money doesn't matter. But thank goodness my varied job resume includes high-end event waitressing, so I've eaten great food. I just told him eclectic, but between us, I like down-home food. Give me a good burger and a shake and I'm there.

He took off for drinks but said we'd do more tomorrow.

That bad part of my brain wants to think he means the horizontal samba, but he doesn't. And I don't want that.

He's just hot.

And it's been a long-ass dry spell.

My roomie, Amber, is out, thank goodness. She's all black curls and big dark eyes and curves that I've seen grown men drool over, not to mention get boners at the wrong time over, especially when she wears one of her clingy, low-cut outfits. So she might not be home tonight. But she's going to want to know what's up with a sudden job change and the rest.

Actually, if someone had asked me yesterday, I'd have balked at the idea of an NDA. Right now, I'm thankful for it.

No one needs to know. Not even my brother, whose business is in trouble.

It's people like my fake fiancé to be that cause those problems in the real estate world. Danny works hard, and sure he's made mistakes and aligned himself with some idiots, but getting a foot in when you're indie is hard.

He needs money to save his business, and he needs me to do so.

Four weeks.

It's only four weeks.

I've had relationships that last longer than that.

Barely.

With that cheerful thought in mind, I will myself to sleep.

I hit the ground running the next morning.

Hudson strikes me as a man who doesn't tolerate tardiness and I'm not about to disappoint him. He's a little scary under the urbane high-end martini of him. Scary like he's a billionaire, and he made that threat. Or promise. Or dire warning. And I'm lying to him. That sort of scary.

I raided Amber's closet for an outfit. One of her more...buttoned up ensembles. On me, it's chic matron. On her, men still no doubt drool. But it's pretty and it had an expensive vibe about it because that girl knows how to find a bargain. I left her a note saying I'll bring it back clean.

After fighting throngs of commuters at the Halsey St. L train stop, then the N train at Union Square, cramming myself in like a sardine, I head to Fifty-Sixth and Fifth Ave and make it to Hudson's office on the top floor with about two minutes to spare.

His gaze is cool and unimpressed and I get the distinct impression I'm late in his eyes.

I smile, and say, "Here for my first day."

"Follow me, Ms. Colton." And he hands his harried receptionist an iPad he's holding.

She barely looks at me as I do as ordered.

The moment the office door swishes shut behind me, I'm encased in silence. Not even the traffic from below, or the noise from outside in the office, penetrates the space.

It strikes me what that means.

"I didn't have my ear to the door," I say. "It was a little open. That's all."

He stares at me and laughs, shaking his head. "I didn't ask."

"It's like the Cone of Silence in here."

"The what?"

"There was this old show and..." I trail off. It occurs to me Sarah might not have sat around watching old *Get Smart* reruns on TV as a kid. Or a teenager. Or last week. "It doesn't matter. It's quiet in here. And—tell me about the job."

Both his eyebrows rise. "Hilarious. I don't have time for this, not today. Here's the NDA and the contract. I have a lawyer to go over it with you—"

"No, I trust you."

Again his eyebrows rise and I refuse to let the fluttering at the pulse in my throat turn into a full on panic attack. I've never had one, but I assume that's what it is. I feel like something's about to explode and my windpipe is getting tighter and I want to run away. But I'm made of sterner stuff than that.

"Okay, Scarlett." He shrugs and hands me a slender folder that's made of the softest leather I've ever touched. It's in a deep mahogany color with a darkly gilded edging. "There's a pen in there, too. My receptionist, Georgina, will give you the tour and settle you in. I'd planned on setting aside time, but I can't. But we'll have dinner."

I almost say you and Georgina, but I'm not sure he appreciates my feeble attempt at humor, so I swallow the words.

He's even more devastating today. The morning light through the wall of glass makes his hair shine with dark chocolate light, and his eyes are the deepest blue. He's wearing a suit in deep charcoal with the finest, most delicate emerald plaid shot through it. I almost sigh but catch myself.

"Dinner?"

"Food? That thing you usually do in the evening? Dinner's a good pretext for going over the things I need you to handle for me personally. I've been promising Georgina to have someone take that part of the work off her plate, and I'll be adding to it." He starts rattling off things at me, but I barely take mental note. "And it's also a great way to start the romance. Wear something good. I'll pick you up at eight."

It's not until I'm done for the day that I realize I never told him where I live.

And it's not until I'm on the train home it hits me in my panic I put down the fancy address Sarah lives at in Manhattan on my forms.

Oh, boy.

Danny's sitting on our sofa, chatting to Amber when I get in. She sees me and rolls her eyes. "I've better clothes, woman."

"Why are you dressed like that?" Danny sets down his Coke and looks at me with a frown.

"A temp job," I say, and then I turn to Amber. "I need a classy outfit. Help."

The plea for help is real because Hudson thinks I live at a *very* fancy Park Avenue South apartment building where Sarah lives. So I need to get there before he does.

Dressed in the peacock blue silk dress Amber swears is pure class, I hastily apply makeup, and Danny crams into the tiny bathroom and frowns behind me.

"Why are you here, anyway?"

"Where are you going?" he counters.

"Out."

"That's not an answer."

"It is. You asked, I answered." I toss my hair, hitting him in the face and then set down the mascara and push him out of the bathroom into the living room. "It's a work thing."

"Well, at least one of us has prospects," he says.

And my heart squishes in. He's my brother and I love him. "It'll get better, Danny. We'll save your business. Build it. And have people coming and wanting places from you."

"I only stopped by because the one place I've got right now is bad. That—" He stops and I know what he was going to say. He was screwed over and that's burned him and his reputation. But that is why I'm doing this. "It's got actual rats. I told the couple not to take it."

"Danny, good for you."

"No. I should have lied."

"You're the last honest realtor out there."

"Yeah, unlike the Sinclairs of the world. Then again, they're loaded."

I bite my lip because I can't tell him. I've signed away everything. But it's for him. "I have to go, but...but trust me, okay?"

And I hope to God those words are true.

Running in heels is not a thing. Whoever thought it was is a demon. But I do it and manage not to fall flat on my face as I hobble-run to the apartment building I'm now pretending is home. My place in Brooklyn isn't going to cut it.

I'm running late because of the trains, and of course, Hudson Sinclair's the type of man who thinks on time is late and that means I'm in deep, deep trouble. He'll find out, and—

I'm here.

The doorman eyes me suspiciously and I go for a smile and a hello, but I'm holding my side, wheezing—you'd think riding about makes me fitter than I am, but...heels. I hold up a finger, trying to get it together when someone appears in front of me.

Every single nerve ending is alight. And the air is suddenly thick and heavy and alive with awareness and I know without looking that it's Hudson.

I look up. Even in heels, I'm nowhere near as tall as him. And I wheeze out a hello.

"You look like you ran a marathon. Traffic held me up. I'm late."

He isn't. He's about five minutes early and by some miracle, I manage to arrive a minute before him. But I nod and wave a hand like I'm letting him off the hook.

"I did some exercise." I take in a breath that is edging towards normal. Only now my heartbeat is erratic because he's there, smelling divine, like that soft leather, honey, and lavender, and I wonder how many women ask if they can lick him, just to see if he tastes as good as he smells. "While I was waiting." I take another breath. "I have to work to keep this up."

I wave a hand down along my body, knowing it's nothing to write home about, but hey, maybe I'm a rich girl with delusions.

Hudson slides a hand under my elbow and I shiver right down to my toes in the shiny stack black heels. My bag bangs against my hip on the other side of me as I stumble. He has magic fingers. They seem to elicit an insane response every time he touches me.

"I thought," he says as our gazes crash and connect, and I almost swear there's humor dancing there in those blue depths, "we could go to Eaton West."

The place is low key, cool, and almost impossible to get into. But then again, most people aren't billionaires.

"That sounds...nice," I say.

"Come on, my car awaits."

And I feel like I'm both tumbling down from a frying pan into a fire and stepping into a fairy tale as we get into the car that pulls up at the sidewalk.

As we pull away, I think, what have I done?

Chapter Five

HUDSON

"No! I can do it!"

Against my better judgement, I'm having drinks after a constructive dinner with Scarlett and enjoying myself.

The conversation meandered as we ate and sipped wine, because knowing all the hard facts in a four-week whirlwind relationship is red flag territory. Getting to know each other on the base level and clicking is more important. The other facts I can get, like anyone, and I'll do that, but this is the foundation, and against the odds, there's something there. A spark I can use, an attraction that's real.

Right now we're in a cozy little bar that's all velvet and leather and low lights near her apartment. It's one of those gems I wouldn't know about, but Ryder does. And it's exactly the perfect mix of laid back and intimate seduction.

"You can't," I say, my fingers loose on my Scotch glass as she ignores her lavender and bergamot martini and tries to tie a cherry stem in her mouth.

I don't think she realizes just how erotic it is. That focus on her soft mouth and rose lips that no longer seem to have lipstick on them. I don't think she knows the thoughts that go through a man's head as he pictures her tongue moving, trying intricate moves in her wet mouth, and what those moves might feel like on his skin, in his mouth, on his cock.

"Damn." She laughs and grabs a napkin and pulls it out. "Maybe I've lost that skill."

"Maybe you never had it at all."

"I might have been very drunk at college when I did it, but I did."

She's fearless. Not in the scale every mountain sense and swim with sharks, but fearless in how she might come across, fearless about the potential of making a fool of herself.

It's guileless, subconscious, and incredibly sexy, and she doesn't even know.

The woman rides about in shiny pants for crying out loud, and she shatters that pampered rich girl mode where looks and presentation and decorum are everything.

I'm aware there are the fame chasers, the outrageous heiresses, but I don't go near that type and she doesn't have that about her, either.

It's just her. Scarlett.

And it's something I can work with.

She leans in and her hand comes down on my thigh. The electric buzz of her touch ignites things inside and I shift a little closer to her because I want to, because I'm compelled to, and because I want to breathe in that flowery green scent of her with that erotic edge I didn't notice earlier.

"Your turn," Scarlett says looking up at me, a smile bringing her face alive in a way that makes my heart thump a little harder.

"Oh hell no, I don't do that shit."

The smile doesn't fade as she leans in a little more, her hand staying where it is and says, "I bet you studied hard and smart, and when you got drunk, you kept it in check. Maybe sowed a few wild oats, but judiciously. And you did everything ahead."

"You have an advantage," I murmur, hooking a lock of her dark honey hair behind her left ear. Her hair is soft as silk and heavier than I thought, while her skin is like satin as my fingers brush against her cheek.

"I do?"

Her breath hitches a little and her pupils dilate and I know she's turned on. It's good, this. It makes everything so much better.

"Yeah," I say, upping the charm a little, because having her where I want her is needed. "Your cousin?"

She frowns, and before she can say a word, my phone buzzes in my pocket and I pull back, finding it a little harder than I should. Compartmentalizing is easy. And this should be easiest of all.

"Oh, fuck."

"You have a secret wife you keep in your attic and she escaped?"

I laugh against my will at her weirdness. Is she quoting one of those Bronte novels? "No. Worse. My mother."

Spoke to Jenson. I'm coming to see you now. Text address.

That's my mother all over. She isn't overly interfering, and for some reason, long after the divorce, she'd turn up to pick up the pieces and hand my father to the next in the line of younger and younger wives. But she isn't to be denied when she decides something, and meeting Scarlett suddenly hit the top of her to-do list.

I check my watch. It's only nine thirty and she lives near here.

"What about her?"

"She wants to meet you."

Scarlett looks completely horrified. "Why would you tell her now?"

"I didn't. I had to sign something for Jenson..." I trail off. Ryder. This place, my mother, it's got him written all over it. I'm going to beat the living shit out of him when I see him next.

It's too early. I know that. I figured since I had four weeks, I'd do the introduction if I had to as close to week four as possible, but then again...if we got it over and done with and my mother put her stamp of approval on this, half the job would be done. Right?

That's if it works.

I eye Scarlett and she eyes me right back. The air is thick with a different sort of tension from the one before.

"Your mother?" she hisses, her fingers digging into my thigh. "Don't you think it's weird as we just met?"

"She believes in love."

"And you don't?"

"Come on, Scarlett. Like you do. This is money, nothing more."

For a moment I think she's going to argue, but the fire that leaps in those hazel eyes dampens and she draws back. "What's love got to do with it, anyway?"

"Just pretend you're besotted."

Scarlett grabs my chin, which I don't think anyone's done since I was five, and drags my face to hers. "How's this for besotted?" And she kisses me.

It's a smack of a kiss that sends all sorts of vibrations rolling through me. Just lips on lips and it's not sexual or romantic but I still react and someone, above the low music I've somehow forgotten is there, clears their throat.

She lets go of me and turns a dark shade of rose.

My mother stands, perfect as always, not overly dressed but on point in a classic black tailored dress and sensible heels. I can't read her expression as she focuses on Scarlett and takes a seat without asking.

"Hudson, be a dear and get me a drink. A mint julep."

I'm about to find a waitress when my mother pins me with a look. "From the bar."

By the time I return, I'm already thinking how to spin this. Ryder's not responding to my texts, which is typical. Weaving through the people to get to the oversize sofa and chair that's tucked in the corner, I see my mother has now taken my place next to Scarlett.

As I sit, my mother takes the drink and barely acknowledges me, which I indulge. After all, it's my mother and I need to play all this close to the bone.

But she's smiling and even laughing with Scarlett, which shocks me a little. Not that my mother laughing is a shock, she's been known to do that, but Scarlett isn't the type of woman I'd normally pick, and I certainly don't introduce them to the woman who birthed me, unless I run into my mother at an event.

"Good to see you having fun," I say, sliding my gaze from one to the other.

My mother's smile turns on me as she takes a sip of her drink. "Your...new PA was telling me some delightful stories about training computers."

Oh Christ. What the actual hell?

But while color flares in Scarlett's cheeks, my mother starts chatting about this and that, different social events coming up that I only ever attend when I have to for business or family obligations. And in those questions are nestled little ones about me and Scarlett.

It could all go terribly, horribly wrong, but it doesn't. Ms. Colton keeps things moving and close to the truth and generic.

When she excuses herself for the bathroom, my mother leans in and says, "Not your usual, Hudson. Maybe you're learning. Tell her we'll have lunch."

I narrow my eyes. "This is a business thing."

"With tongues?" She smiles again, cat-like this time, her carefully made-up eyes crinkling. "Far be it from me to lecture you on mixing business and pleasure, Hudson. But make sure it's worth it."

And with that, she leaves.

I've no idea if I've won a round or what, but one thing's for sure, my mother knows about the letter and that means I need to play things very carefully.

After all, I want that inheritance. It's mine.

It doesn't take long to settle back into the easy conversation with Scarlett, and even though I don't want to, I have to end the evening. So I walk her home. It's a slow walk through the park where the lights draw the lovers out.

"You survived."

"Dinner and drinks, or you?" she asks, matching her steps to my longer one.

I arch a brow at her and pull her out of the way of a cyclist. "My mother."

"She seems nice." She pauses. "Scary, but nice. I guess now I know where you get it from."

"Which part?" My hand brushes hers and I want to thread my fingers with hers, bring her closer against me. I don't.

She lifts a hand to brush hair out of her face that the night breeze sends there, the warmth of the air tinged with a cool touch, and she half smiles. "Definitely the scary part."

I'm telling myself the only reason I didn't want to end the evening, and the only reason we're walking so slow, is because every minute counts. Time is short. Time is money. And I have a lot I want to get done.

It's not just my share of the jewels, it's the piece of the Sinclair legacy in the family business. I have power and money, but these are things I can't buy and this woman next to me is my ticket to get what I want.

That's the reason, and no other.

We come out of the park and onto Park Avenue South and finally her building is there. I stop near the entrance, close enough she doesn't have far, and distant enough there are shadows that cloak.

There's a point of no return coming, and my mother's appearance tonight brings it into sharp focus. I have a few days, maybe a week, in which I can't choose someone else. I'd have to change my plans slightly if I do, either keep Scarlett on with the job or fire her, but at that point, it's null and void. I'd find another woman, and have this as just a flirtation and nothing more.

My mind ticks with ideas and ways to be smart about it if things go askew. But I'm hoping not.

We click, and that's a big push in the right direction.

"Well," she says, looking up at me. "Thanks for everything."

I'm suddenly aware this is the time when one of us should suggest going upstairs if this was something else.

"What was the thing about computers?"

Scarlett frowns. "Oh. I saw...I saw a program on training AIs and I told her how fascinating it was."

I laugh. "She was probably beyond relieved you weren't talking about fashion shows and the Hamptons."

And then Scarlett does something unexpected. She rises up to brush her mouth against my cheek.

Her lips are softer than the smack on the mouth she gave me at the bar. Soft and warm and something I want to taste.

I don't think. I slide my hands up her arms and hold her, my gaze colliding with hers. Those hazel depths are liquid and full of something that looks like desire.

So I do it. I brush my mouth against hers in a teasing taste of a kiss.

And she moans. A soft little sound. And it calls to me.

This time it isn't about thinking or not thinking. It's just feeling.

"I'm going to kiss you again," I say, running a thumb over her lips, parting them, "thoroughly."

Once more, I lower my mouth to hers.

Chapter Six

SCARLETT

Oh my sweet, sweet Lord.

This man can kiss.

His mouth is hot and wet and firm on mine, and tendrils of desire bloom like insane flowers inside me.

The first kiss was divine, but this is a game changer. It's seduction, it melts my bones, and my heart is hammering in my chest as he draws me into him. I'm wrapped around him, his erection pressing against my stomach though he makes no move to do anything but kiss.

I'm burning. I'm pure sensation and I want to go deeper and deeper into the kiss to see where it goes. My clit throbs with need as my insides clench, like there's something they must have. That pleasure-filled desire is blooming madly and if I could crawl into this kiss, I would. Right down into its depths.

There are songs written about kisses, books. Movies made. Legends built and this kiss blows them all into nothing more than dust.

And I'm melting into him. His tongue is magic in my mouth and he tastes like Scotch and sin and wicked promises.

His hand slides down my spine, a soft, tantalizing touch I feel everywhere, and then the kiss is over and he's let me go.

I'm a mess. I'm panting. I thought running earlier was my undoing, but really, it's this. My blood pounds loudly in my ears and my entire body is encased in some kind of heat haze that the running could only dream of creating. And inside, down deep in my core, right there between my legs, I'm a throbbing, needing, mass of nerve ends that are tight and aching in that good way I know his touch can both rile and soothe and push me over the edge and he—

Hudson Sinclair looks cucumber cool and spectacularly unruffled, like he didn't just have the kiss of his life.

I hit the concrete hard. Metaphorically, that is. Reality floods my veins with a coolness that a vat of ice never could.

For all I know, Hudson wasn't moved by that kiss like I am. Or was. I'm over it now. At least, that's what I tell myself. He's rich, he dates the kind of gorgeous women I could never hope to be. And he thinks I'm some airhead rich girl who can't hold on to money.

I thought I was wildly attracted to him before, but that was mere passing fancy. This is a drop your panties attraction. That kiss opened something in me.

But not for him, because this is fake. And now he's staring at me. I have to say something. "That was...nice."

His eyebrows rise and I want to melt away.

"It's good," I say, "to know we can do that in case we have to. For...appearances."

Hudson's mouth quirks a little. "Do you want me to walk you in?"

"God no!" I stop and a woman walking by casts me a long look. I ignore her, just like I ignore the burn in my cheeks that's all embarrassment. "People will talk."

What I want is for him to kiss me again. I think about doing it, just to see if that was a fluke, but I don't have the nerve. Besides, I'm horribly aware I don't live in the building behind me and I'm lying to the man who said he'd destroy me if I do that.

I don't think he will, but there's that martini quality to him. The bite beneath the smooth that worries me.

It's not like he's going to find out, but I'd rather not test that, so I step away and say, "I'll see you tomorrow at work. For you."

And then, because he's making no effort to move from where he stands, looking all relaxed and gorgeous and unruffled, I whirl around and head to the building before I can think about it.

I bound up through the big door where the doorman stands in his natty suit and hat and I say, "I'll give you twenty bucks if you let me go inside for five minutes."

I ended up giving that doorman—Fred his name is—a cool fifty for letting me do that. When I came out, I peered up and down the street and Fred said the gentleman had gone.

With a wave, I'd taken off, hobbling down the street to the subway station because now that adrenaline had ebbed away, my feet hurt like I'd performed some kind of torture on them.

Now I'm in bed, my covers up under my chin and Mr. Figglesmort in a death grip. He's used to it, and I need the comfort from the old bear.

I try to sleep and can't, so by the time morning comes I drag myself out of bed and into the shower like I drank ten of those terrible martinis—actual martinis, not Hudson type martinis—instead of half of one.

"You look like you had a night."

Amber is pointing a perfectly manicured finger at me in an accusing fashion and I swallow hard, wishing I'd stayed in bed, but she's not usually up at six a.m., even on a work morning. She has one of those hipster jobs that starts at eleven.

"I have a night each time the sun goes down," I say, scurrying into our tiny kitchen and searching for sustenance. There are Cheerios, which I hate, but I grab a handful and crunch them down dry, anyway.

She crosses her arms, blocking the door. "Oh, very funny. Who is he?"

"Who's what now?"

"The man you keep borrowing my clothes for."

"I'm not. There is no man."

But heat is burning in my face again and she gives a triumphant, "Hah! Liar! Tell me all...or I won't let you wear that."

I look down. "This is mine."

"Hmm... Cute little black pants, perfect for boots or strappy heels and a poppy red blouse with a black pussy bow. Are you sure?"

"Yes. You made me buy these because you said every girl needs an outfit that's office chic and ready to party on the down low. Whatever that means."

She narrows her eyes at me. "You're trying to change the subject."

"I have a new job. It pays well. That's all."

"There's a man. I can tell."

"You always think there's a man," I snap, taking another handful of Cheerios and nabbing her overly sweet coffee that's sitting on the bench and take a big swallow. It's warm because she forgot it and it's creamy and sweet and very caffeinated, so I drink some more. "But..."

I stop talking.

"I knew it," Amber says. "Who is he?"

"It's not...it's not like whatever you're thinking. It's to do with work."

She clutches a hand to her generous breasts. "You're a high-class hooker. I should have known when you started taking my clothes."

"Are you saying you wear high-class hooker clothes?"

"Hey, they do very well."

"I'm not." And with that I hand her the coffee and push past with words of trains and running late and new boss and hard ass.

I know I didn't get away with it, not really. Amber's got her claws out for the story and she knows there's one. But I can't tell her anything.

This is way more complicated than I thought.

I don't have time over the next few days to do anything but panic. I'm in the deep end, and as a boss, Hudson is scary.

He's not an ogre. But he's exacting and he demands excellence in everything. Right to the smallest detail.

When I said hard ass to Amber, I didn't know how wrong I was.

He was worse.

Steel and ice ran in his veins, and no one dared to put a foot wrong around him.

No wonder he's paying me so much. This is Gulag-style work. But with pay. It's like back breaking but for the mind. And the worst thing? The absolute worst? He holds himself to the highest of all standards.

I saw a grown man cry. Not when Hudson was looking, but after he came to tell him that he'd screwed something up. And Hudson hadn't said anything other than okay.

It was worse than being reamed or fired.

And me?

I have no idea what I'm doing. I'm in the deep end and I'm teaching myself to swim.

I'm getting ready to leave, but I have to send an email to one of his clients who wants a meeting. And for some reason, this woman is the worst. She's demanding and pushy and she's also very, very rich, so I'm not sure why she's at the bottom of the pile.

Perhaps that's why he needs a PA.

I live in a cavern next to his office. I'm like a side step to his receptionist. I'm about to press send on the email when the pressure in the room changes and my skin starts to buzz.

Without looking, I know he'd stepped inside.

Hudson approaches the desk of blackwood where I sit. It's some designer piece, all curved and beautiful and I'm sort of in love with it. With my cavern, actually. It's bright and filled with black steel and white and creams and dark, black woods.

My brain is melting because he's there. He's changed from his suit and is dressed head to toe in black and looks impossibly suave and dangerous in that impeccable way, and he's so gorgeous I'm probably drooling.

"Scarlett," he says, his voice soft and velvety. "You have a…a way of working that's unique."

"Thank you?"

He smiles. "Yesterday, you booked two meetings for me at the same time. One in Queens and one in SoHo. I'm good, but even I haven't mastered time travel or cloning. Try to keep an eye on that." He sits on my desk and crosses his legs, his gaze skimming over me and then to the computer where my hand still hovers over the keyboard.

"I'm so sorry. I didn't mean that. I thought it was the following week for the Queens meeting." His face doesn't change, but I know that's the wrong answer. "The follow up meeting. I'll call and fix it. Send an edible arrangement."

He just nods and says, "Okay."

I know exactly why that man cried in the corner of one of the offices. That okay is horrible. I don't know how or why, but it is. I'd rather he scream at me.

"Also..." His hand is holding my wrist, his thumb drawing circles against the sensitive skin there and I'm having trouble thinking of anything but that. "I'd rather you not press send on this email."

"Okay. Is she your girlfriend?"

He looks completely horrified and he actually shudders. "No. Let's just say while I want her money, I don't want anything that comes with it."

"You could—"

"The meetings thing is your one screw up. Now." He lets me go like he didn't just threaten the job. I want to ask if that threat includes our contract, but I'm not that brave. "Come on. We have things to do tonight."

"Now?"

"That's what tonight means."

"I can't."

"Why not?" He stands. "This is part of our contract, or didn't you read that? I need you when I need you. We have four weeks, not months."

Shit, I have plans with my brother that I can't get out of. Anything else, for anything else with him, I'd cancel, but I promised I'd go to an event with him this evening that's important and I can't let him down.

"It's just..." It's on the tip of my tongue to say I've plans with my brother, but Sarah's an only child, so I panic. "I've got a charity event. It's the Matronly Matrons of the Hamptons fundraiser. It's this thing where—"

"That's fine." He cuts me off and I'm almost sagging with relief because I honestly don't know where that would have ended.

"Tomorrow. No excuses."

I watch him leave, hating the disappointment that surges at his departure. Instead, I delete the email and shut down the computer and head to meet my brother.

This all has the beginnings of a nightmare. Especially how the little lies keep growing into more lies. But this is only four weeks. And I can control an unrequited crush for four weeks. Right? I can do that. Four weeks. Then I get paid. Then I can save my brother's business and help him find his confidence again, and I never have to think about this job. Except when I'm old and gray. Then I can relish the memory of the kiss.

But I just have to do this for four weeks.

What, really, could possibly go wrong?

Chapter Seven

HUDSON

I'm more pissed off than I'd like to admit.

Normally it wouldn't bother me, but after the kiss the other day, the kiss that still comes to me like the scent of skin at different times, it's something that bites deep.

I don't know what the fuck this fundraiser was, and I've no desire to find out. Those kinds of things bore the crap out of me. But for some reason, since I've gotten to know her, at least as much as I can in a few days, I would have thought she'd hate that kind of event.

My home is blessedly quiet, and nowhere near where most people think I'd live. It's in the quiet mid upper east side of Manhattan, the street is tree lined and the houses worth a fortune. And mine, well, it's a lovely brownstone with five floors, but I've got the top two as my private domain.

The rest is for guests and entertaining if I choose to do so, which is only usually for business purposes, but I'm here to sleep and eat and fuck in the master bedroom that's not my room. That's when I bring them here.

The event tonight would have been made more interesting with Scarlett, which surprises me. I was only planning to take her for the purposes of our contract, but she's a bright light, full of life I didn't know I liked having around. The stuffy suits of the company I just bought bored the pants off me and I stayed as long as was polite.

Now I'm home, some old school blues on because that's my mood, and Scotch.

All I want is to relax and think about my plans.

So that's when my phone rings. I pick it up from the arm of the chair in the living room in my private quarters and sigh, hitting answer and speaker at the same time.

"Hello, Mother."

"Hudson. I've been speaking with Jenson. And I think I should bring up a few things if this girl turns into something more than just your employee…"

The next morning, everything at the office is running smoothly, the way I expect it to. Even my faux fiancée is hard at work. Of course, her idea of work and mine seem to differ. It's not wrong, per se, but it's not good.

I sit behind my desk and place the new contract on my desk, staring at it. The reason I'm late.

If things were perfect, then I'd be talking to her right now instead of sitting in here.

I want excellence.

I demand it.

No one's going to believe I'd hire her if she didn't give me that. She's not the package I go for, so she needs to be on her game to make it all work.

Yes, I'm being hard, and perhaps I'm incorrect with not good.

Scarlett's green.

She's probably done a version of this job, but I have to face facts—even a struggling woman from old money is still a socialite, and that goes for struggling women from old money who don't seem to fit the mold.

Still.

Green.

I'm going to have to spend some time going over this in every tiny detail so she can do the job I want. I might as well do that if I'm going to stick with this thing. We're not even done with week one and I have a new contract already.

My mother last night…

I'm not sure if she's playing me for her own reasons or if she's trying to make sure I protect myself. Along with the family name.

She might not have been born a Sinclair, but she is one, through and through. And she has a point about making sure if I choose a bride to be sure. Some might see that as a be sure that you love them, but I see it as taking care that everything is covered.

I don't want to pass that goal post and have it fall apart because of Scarlett. And if Scarlett balks at the new NDA and contract, then I have time to find someone else.

Actually, if she does, I can use her unusual PA skills as a reason why things end.

It's a win-win for me.

My mind at ease, I call her into my office.

She's a pretty deer in headlights.

I'm not really sure why I think that since there's nothing deer-like about her. But that's what she is right now. She knows something is up.

"Sit." I wave at the sofa and she perches on it like she did only a few days ago.

I take the seat next to her and place the folder between us.

"My mother called when I got home last night."

"You're close then?" She blinks. "Not implying anything...Oedipal."

That startles a laugh at me. "Not my type."

"My mouth sometimes does what it wants, I'm sorry."

Nerves are surging into life inside me, which is weird. I don't ever get nervous. Then again, I don't ever have my desires riding on a woman I don't know who tastes like heaven laced with promises of all kinds of deliciously dark and carnal acts I shouldn't be thinking about.

"Scarlett." I'm trying to get the words that ran so smoothly before her lithe self walked in. "We need to talk."

Her cheeks turn a dusty rose and she looks at me. "It was one mistake yesterday—"

"Not that, but since you bring it up, I get it. You probably cruised by before on your family name. And XO provides stellar temps, but the office work there isn't at the level I demand. We'll spend time on how to handle certain aspects of my business life later today." If there's a later, but I keep that to myself. "No. I want to talk about this."

I hand her the folder and she opens it, our fingers brushing and a cascade of awareness bursts inside me from that touch, sending fantasies of fucking her on the sofa racing through my brain.

She's frowning as she's flipping through the pages and I'm positive her mind hasn't gone where mine has. Thank goodness. Because I don't need the added complications of that.

"I signed this stuff—" She stops, bites her lip as she clearly catches on. "A year?"

"As I said, there was something my mother said about it. Not that she knows about this." I point to her and me and the contract. "But if I were to fall in love and find a bride in four weeks, then I can bet there's a forfeit if it ends right after. So, I figured we stay engaged on paper for a year and then it can go south."

"That's a lot more than four weeks."

"You don't have to sign. You don't have to do anything you don't want, Scarlett. But it is a lot of money, and I'll pay more. I just need to protect my own interests here."

"Oh, God..."

She says this so quietly I almost don't catch it and I'm not sure what the problem is. Unless there's a man somewhere on her horizon.

I tap my foot on the floor. "If this doesn't fit in with your plans, then I'll find someone else. We'll work out a percentage for the last few days and call it a day."

She doesn't say a word and I push to my feet. I'm not playing. I'm not bluffing. She needs the money, but so do others out there.

"Wait."

I look at her and do just that.

She's biting her lip, her brow is creased into a frown, and she looks like there's a world speeding in circles in her head.

"If there's a guy you're seeing, or after, then that's your business, but anything needs to be kept very quiet outside this four-week period. If you're going to sign."

"What if you meet someone?"

"I'm able to keep it in my pants and I'm not looking for a relationship. I don't believe in them, and I certainly don't believe in the fairy tale called love."

"That's sad."

"If you do, then you're deluded. Relationships that claim love end in divorce and then the next one and the next one, and I'd rather not mess with that shit. And this thing with you and me, fake as it is, is already one hell of a headache. I can only imagine the real deal. No thanks."

She shrugs and takes a step back. "A year. It's...that's a long time. If we can't talk about it, then...what about family? Friends?"

"They can't know the truth. Let's get through the four weeks."

"That doesn't work." Scarlett looks like the floor is going to open up and eat her because she spoke to me like that. "It works, I just...there are people."

"What people?"

Panic crosses her face, and she grips the contract tight. "Just. People. Don't you have friends?"

"I have colleagues. Old friends. Brothers." I don't keep up with anyone except family and those who can make my business tick and earn money, but that's not her business.

"I have friends. And people ask things. I...I do things. You know, like the matron's charity. And if—"

"This pans out after four weeks, I'll get you a fucking ring you can sell after twelve months."

"I don't want that."

Her voice is a little thready, and she's breathing in short, sharp inhalations.

I don't know what the problem here is, and for some reason this is more complicated in her head, which makes me want to take a closer look at her and all she is.

"I just mean, if I have an NDA and we can't tell anyone, then it's also going to look suspicious."

"You have a point. We'll discuss it in a week or two. If you still want to do it."

She stalks up to me and I'm immediately surrounded by hints of flowers. "Why not now?"

"Because I'm private."

But she has a point. If we run into people, we can't just say nothing. There are events and places to go, and while the contract says no media and the NDA says not to tell anyone the truth, there's nothing about close friends and family and where appropriate.

"I'm not planning on getting a billboard," she says.

"Okay. Need to know on a new relationship. When it gets quote unquote serious, we can then look at the perimeters. There's room for that in the contract."

"Oh."

"Oh," I mimic. Then, when she snatches the contracts back to her, I hold out a pen and she signs, muttering things to herself. Then she shoves it all at me. "Is that all?"

I slide my gaze over her. "No. Dress up tonight. We're going out."

Chapter Eight

SCARLETT

A year.

That's so different to four weeks. I mean, I know he wanted to make some changes, but I thought that happened to be rules. He's a guy who seems happy with rules. A hot, sexy, rule man.

But a year and a new contract and NDA?

This drags me in deep, right down into the tangled mire of it all. And I have a problem. With four weeks, lying about my name…or who I am isn't going to be much on any grand scale. Hot, sexy rule man threats aside.

But a year…

I drag in a breath as I drag a dress off a hanger and hold it against myself in my bedroom mirror. Rolling my eyes at the sight, I toss it on the bed and grab another.

The thing is, a year is a bunch of four weeks. That's a whole load of things going wrong, or the potential, and what if he loses everything and then not only destroys me, but Danny?

I pause, my throat closing up and panic cutting into me with little barbed strands.

Okay, I'm totally panicking here, but I had to sign. If I'd walked away, I... My shoulders slump as I drop the dress. If I'd walked away now, then he still might do all that, like he said, and I'd also end up with nothing.

Danny would have nothing. All his hopes and dreams that are already battered would be destroyed.

And I'm smart. I know that. There's a way to do this. Sarah won't be back for a while, not according to the breezy text I got. We're not the closest of friends, but we're good. So even if she does come back, Hudson doesn't seem to be in her world of parties and glitterati and the like.

I'll have time to think it all through and make it to the end.

With that thought firmly in my head, I leave my room to raid Amber's closet.

After all, I've got a not date I know nothing about to prepare for.

I get there with minutes to spare.

Hudson texted me to meet him. And I'm so pleased I chose upscale clothes that are probably from my roomie's funerals and future mother-in-law's lunch date collection. As in something that's going to fit in anywhere and not show too much skin.

That was the plan, anyway, and considering my attributes aren't as out there as hers, I think I pull off the deep chocolate dress and low heels which are mine. As is the Kate Spade knock off I got that I swear looks just like the OG.

I'm programming his name into my phone as Martini Legend when a shiver passes through me and all my senses go into overdrive as I stand outside the SoHo building.

I don't need to look up to know Hudson is there. He moves in close. I'm still staring at the screen of my phone, my fingers biting into the protective cover, trying to gain some semblance of calm.

He's so there, close enough he brushes against me, and I stare up into those dark eyes and forget to breathe, all over again.

"Should I even ask?"

His voice slides through me, and I'm lost in those eyes, in him, until someone bumps into me with a hurried apology and drags me out of whatever world I went and put myself in.

"What do you mean?"

"The name?" His eyebrow rises as he nods at the screen of my phone.

I laugh, a weird relief washing over me. "You said keep it secret."

"I'm thinking there's a story, and I'm both curious and not sure I want to know." Then his mouth is at my ear and little electric pulses dart along my spine at the whisper of his breath there. "You look good, Scarlett."

The latent heat in his words coils around me and I want to say the same to him, but who am I kidding? This man always looks incredible. He can ignite fantasies just by walking into a room.

"Thank you."

Hudson straightens up and offers me his arm. "Shall we?"

I still have no idea what this is. The building is beautiful, classic, an icon of the cast iron district's past. But it isn't a restaurant or shop, and it doesn't look like some fancied up apartment building.

He leads the way. "I own this building, and we'll be meeting with a who's who of the real estate world. More or less. And clients. So do try and keep your mouth under some semblance of control."

"Me? I'm the modicum of decorum and restraint." At the narrowed eyed look he gives me accompanied by the low slung smile that says I'm lying, I fight the urge to step on his foot. "And I promise I'll only call you Mr. Martini Legend once."

"Just try."

"I will." I won't. I don't want his wrath upon me. Whatever that might entail.

The door opens, and it's an unassuming one. I mean, it's a door. But what's beyond takes my breath.

A beautiful space awaits of polished floors and wide openness that during the day would let in light, especially the higher up you went with each floor. It's elegant, tasteful, modern, and yet keeps the charm and history of the building with the exposed beams and arched windows.

I know enough about real estate in New York to know this will probably be sold or rented as a home, and where we are would be the great room if one wanted to put in walls. But right now, it was set up as a playground for an architect and interior designer, and as I took in the people and the discreet staff, a perfect place for some kind of party.

In my head, I go over the emails I took care of that day and realize some of them were for this. The rest would have been in the hands of his receptionist, Georgina, but the people he wanted here I was in charge of—so to speak—in getting here…at different times. And I hope to God I got it all correct.

His hand is on my lower back. It's both disconcerting and comforting and I don't know how it can be like that except it is.

My part is simple as we move about the room. Let him chat and get him to the people he wants to talk to and get him out of the conversations he doesn't.

At first I'm shit at it. A little loud or abrupt, but the pressure of his hand changes and gives me the clues I need. And I'm good at that. Learning fast and adapting. It comes with having to do a million different jobs to make money over the years to keep our little family—mine and Danny's—afloat. And with my love of training AIs.

When Hudson talks to someone he wants to, his hand isn't there on my back. But when he's done, it's there. Sometimes hard, sometimes soft.

So, I wing it. I'll jump into conversations to give him an out. I'll pretend there's something we need to take care of work related—cell phones are a godsend as long as you remember to keep yours on silent.

This is industry as well as those interested in having this space. And I know there are people here hungry to work for Hudson. Or even poach someone who can't afford his asking price.

Danny would love this. I want to text him, but I can't. I mean, what a mess that would all be. So, I keep going, keep smiling and keep longing for when Hudson touches my lower back and murmurs in my ear which person he'd like to talk to next.

Oh, who needs sweet nothings when they have that?

I grab hold of myself as I grab a glass of wine from a passing waiter. This is all pretend. I need to remember that.

Hudson's talking to some impossibly glamorous woman and hasn't glanced at me once. And she's loaded. Used to power and commanding it. I can see that in how she owns the place. Except him. He doesn't react to her any differently than he does the waiter or anyone else.

Secretly, my inner bitch likes that.

I have problems.

"A penny for them?"

I whirl around and almost spill my drink on the too-handsome man standing there. He's in a lovely suit, but not up to Hudson's standards and he's the kind of good looking that I suspect takes him hours to perfect. But I smile because right now I'm out of the boat and in the water and Hudson isn't there to steer me, so for all I know this guy's important.

"Oh, just enjoying the evening," I say, taking a gulp of the wine.

He smiles the kind of dazzling smile that came from a dentist with a psychotic love of whitener. "I haven't seen you before. Are you one of us?"

I don't know what that means. "I'm—"

"We should get out of here. I don't think Sinclair's going to talk to us this evening." The smile doesn't fade, just turns hard. "Not the little people."

"I work for him, so I don't think—" I stop. "I don't think he'd appreciate that. If you'll excuse me."

I whirl away from him and start heading back to Hudson, who's watching me with narrowed eyes. Or maybe he's looking at someone else because he's back talking to the woman. And I breathe a sigh of relief.

A short-lived one.

Because there, to my left, is someone I know.

Danny.

Shit. I cast a glance at Hudson because my brother's heading over, but Hudson isn't paying me attention. So, I grab Danny's arm and drag him off to a corner.

"What the hell are you doing here?" Danny frowns at me.

"Danny," I hiss. "You—"

"Oh my fucking God." He's not looking at me. He's looking over my shoulder.

I turn.

My brother clutches my arm. "Hudson Sinclair's coming this way."

Chapter Nine

HUDSON

Of course, the moment I need my less than on point PA slash fake fiancée she's not there.

No. She's apparently making the rounds and picking up men.

And I, for one, am not fucking happy.

She leans in, touching the young guy on the arm in a familiar way that spikes a strange, harsh sensation through my blood. And she says something to him and then hurries over, almost running into me.

There are enough people at my exclusive event where I'm dabbling in some head hunting and showing off this building to an array of wanna-be buyers. I'm not selling yet. Just whetting appetites, letting them glimpse the possibilities for this place, and weeding out those I don't want to have their fingers on it.

I want my hands on Scarlett. I know that. I shouldn't want that, but I do.

But this isn't about lust. This is about how things look, or will look. We're keeping things quiet for obvious reasons, but she needs to play the game I've set or else she's useless to me. Worse than useless.

Thing is, as the cold, stark anger threads through me, I'm not Mr. Nice Guy. I've got morals and I pay well, but cross me and I'm like my brothers, like my father. I will destroy you.

I warned her, but that bouncy, bubbly personality might not let her see me for what I am.

Fuck, I fired four people and destroyed a company today. The people weren't up to the job and the company was small and in my way and a complete and utter waste of space.

I'm not one of those people who squash the little players for fun or because I can. Diversity is the name of the game, and I don't play in the small real estate arenas. But start poaching on my territory and you are fucking dust.

And she's doing that. Right now. Poaching other men. Disrupting the delicate ecosystem I'm creating.

Without another thought, I cross to her. I don't weave through the people, they get the fuck out of my way.

"What are you doing, Scarlett?" I don't even spare the guy a look. At all. He's nothing to me and she's about to join him in utter obscurity—I don't care who or what her family is, either—if she's not careful.

She stared up at me and something twisted deep in my guts, hard and I've never wanted to strangle such a pretty, slender neck before. Nor rearrange a guy's face I don't want to look at.

I'm not going to do it. Too many witnesses. Besides, we have a contract.

"Scarlett?"

She swallows, her eyes way too big and her mouth opening and closing.

"Five seconds, or I walk."

"Look, you—"

"Danny," she says, her gaze flitting to the guy, her hand going for his arm again. But she only gave it a quick squeeze before she dropped it back to her side. "Don't."

"Scarlett," the guy with a death wish says, "what's going on?" His gaze cut to Hudson and I finally look at him.

Blonde, shorter than me, but good looking enough, I suppose. Dressed up, but in a suit that came right off the rack. Not like some of those who I allow to finagle their way in that I swear shop at some bargain basement, but off the rack. I normally don't tend to judge because talent is talent, and I'm willing to take on rough diamonds here and there. But this one?

I don't like him.

Don't trust him.

There's something familiar about him I can't put my finger on and that irks me. So do the light brown eyes I suspect usually sparkle with friendliness, but now look at me in suspicion.

He starts to reach out his hand and Scarlett jumps in front of me, tugging me away.

I'm so surprised she's doing such a thing I let her.

We don't get far before I sweep her up against me, fingers biting down on the soft warmth of her arm. "Who the fuck is that?"

She swallows.

"You know, Scarlett, I can be nice if I choose and I can also be a complete callous bastard. Don't bring that out in me. You won't enjoy it."

I stop, struggling to get hold of the strange heavy thing that twists inside me.

"Hudson." Her voice is soft and sweet and beguiling and I narrow my eyes.

She can't find the words. That's obviously because she has someone here. No...she wouldn't dare. This guy, this Danny, has just turned up.

"We have a contract." I want to tell her she can fuck whomever she wants behind closed doors, but I can't seem to say those words. Hypocritical maybe, considering that's my plan and has been since we launched into this a few days ago, but while I'm horny, it's not for anyone else. "Your public little get-togethers with love interests are a no go, understood?"

She breathes out and her shoulders slump down a little like the tension vibrating has gone.

"I'm sorry," she said, dipping her head down along with her gaze in a picture of demure innocence I don't quite believe. "I didn't know he'd be here. I'll talk to him—"

"No." My tone barks a little louder than I'd like and her head jerks up, spots of color lighting her cheeks. She's enough to steal my breath.

"No," I repeat, a little cooler and calmer. "Just get rid of him. We have to be careful, that's all." I flick a glance at the Rolex. "You have a minute to tell him to get lost. I've got people I want you to meet. And, you're working."

Satisfied, I pull out my phone and send a text to myself about something that's come to me. Work soothes. And time is money.

She's back at my side in less than a minute and that heavy twisting thing abates and I've a horrible feeling as I lead her away that it just might be jealousy.

Which is ridiculous.

"It's all fine," she says, way too cheerily in that way that almost verges on hysteria.

Someone nearly bumps into her in their haste to get to me—one reason why when I have these things I usually only send my top people. I'm here because I do need to be seen occasionally, and it's a good opportunity to be seen with her without being seen in a splashy or overt way—and I pull her out of the way.

I leave my hand on her lower back, just to make sure she stays out of the way of others and to let her know when I need to end this conversation, and it's the only reason.

I chat to the man, and she's warm and her scent wafts around me. A subtle thing that makes me want to sniff it out, find the source. Maybe she applied perfume on that sweet spot right behind her earlobe. Or perhaps it's at the base of her throat, or even in between her softly rounded breasts—

Calmly, I shift my mind to the conversation, which is so damn boring it kills any ideas my dick might have of spontaneously growing a boner.

The guy is in his sixties, portly, with a bald pate and natty gray goatee and his gaze keeps shifting to Scarlett, like she's a party favor.

He wants to invest. I don't need the money, but he has influence in certain arenas in real estate where he can help open doors.

I'd like the smart route to those doors, but if he keeps eyeing Scarlett's breasts I'm going to find another way.

"Actually," I say, cutting him off, "I need to discuss some things with my PA. If you don't mind."

With that, I press my hand firmly against her back and steer her away, and to the back of the room where I grab a whiskey and glance at her.

She's frowning. "Did you just rudely cut that old bore off because he was looking at me like he wanted to lick me?"

"What gave you that idea?" I take a swallow of the peaty liquid and it heats a path through my blood. But it's not as hot as her.

She grabs herself a drink, too. We're at the little bar tucked way in the back that's basically a refill station for the waitstaff. But they know who I am and wouldn't dare say a word.

"Because you were rude."

My mouth twitches as humor starts to bubble inside. "Maybe I'm rude to everyone."

"I don't think so. I mean, you probably are, but on the surface you're a martini. It's not until later all that smoothness moves in for the kill, and then it's too late."

"Is that the reason you programmed my name in like that?"

It's a small smile. Like a cat, and my reaction is innate. I shift closer to her, an electric thrill running through me. "You should watch it."

She's scared of me, but not when the air is alive with heat and the crackling awareness between us. When it's like that, she's excited. But I don't mind, so am I. Scarlett has a habit of sliding in when you don't notice, even when the only thing in the room you can see and smell is her.

If I'm a martini, then she's smoke; elusive and scented and the perfect accompaniment.

If you were so inclined.

If you were someone who believed in where this could lead.

"You like to play with fire, Scarlett," I murmur, dipping my head close.

The only place this goes is light flirtation. For show.

Regardless of that pull on the senses she has.

She raises her head and her hazel eyes are almost dark gold the way her hair gleams in the low, buttery light in the space. And especially in the low-lit corner we occupy.

"Maybe I like fire."

I want to taste the lips, take the invitation that's there, just beneath the surface.

Shifting a little, our bodies brush and a small gasp escapes her as I lower my head.

"Fuck, Hudson, and they call me a player."

Raising my gaze, I narrow my eyes at Ryder.

"There's a thing called timing."

"Yeah, and I have that in buckets." He gives me an innocent look. "What? I didn't say it was good timing for others, but...for me, it's always fantastic. I'm Ryder, Hud's brother."

"Do you ever cross the streams?" Scarlett says, taking his hand.

Ryder kisses it in a practiced, smarmy way I don't like and he laughs.

"The what?" I say.

"He's not really one for decadence."

"Ghostbusters is decadent?" Scarlett asks Ryder, but she gives me a curious look.

The mood is ruined and I'm not sure if I should be thanking my erstwhile brother or beating him up.

Ryder holds her hand until he catches my glare, then holds it a little longer, just to piss me off. Which is working.

"If it doesn't make him money or build a better business," Ryder says, "or streamline his life into even more efficiency, if possible, then it's decadent. Actually, are you sure you're not secretly German?"

"What are you on about?" I check my watch and it's really time for me to get out of here.

Ryder shrugs. "They're known for their efficiency and—"

"I'm not sure if that's racist or just a jackass kinda generalization that comes out of your mouth," I say. Then I turn to Scarlett, who's watching this with way too much interest. "We should get out of here."

Ryder's eyebrows rise. "Well now, just wait until I tell Magnus and Kingston about this, they'll—"

"This is Scarlett, my new PA."

"Who is going to do the rounds once," she says, looking a little unsure, but Ryder nods and gives her the thumbs up, "and see if there's anyone I should contact tomorrow for you."

And then she's off and Ryder's grinning at me. He crosses his arms over his chest. "Well, well, well, that's a pretty little cat for your ugly ass pigeon to chase."

"I...I don't even know where to start with that."

"Hey, there you are." Magnus says, after striding across the room. "Who was that?"

"That was his new PA." Ryder's an ass.

Magnus doesn't say much, just nods. "You're doing it?"

"Yes." But right then I see something that makes my blood hot like the sun.

Scarlett and that guy called Danny.

"I'll talk to you both later."

And then I make my way over to where Scarlett is with the guy. Too close. Too familiar. Too touchy-feely.

It hits me. What the feeling is. The realization makes my blood burn hotter.

Fuck.

I'm jealous.

And I'm going to do something about it.

Chapter Ten

SCARLETT

My life is suddenly like I'm a dancer. One who does that complicated ballroom stuff. Like the tango. Except I've never had any lessons and I've been thrown in amongst the world's best.

I do the rounds, collect cards, make promises for appointments, and all the time I'm trying to get out of there.

Hudson says we're leaving. Us.

And oh my God. Are all his brothers hot as fuck? Because it's two for two so far. There are five of them. All big, all probably gorgeous, and all richer and scarier than the devil.

But Hudson...oh, that moment back there in the corner, tucked by the service bar. I'm not even sure I'd call what happened flirting. Maybe more like some seductive foreplay and all our clothes were on and sex was never mentioned. My cheeks are hot. They're pure flame, and—

"Scarlett!"

"Jesus, Danny," I hiss, trying to shake him off. "I thought you left."

"Are you crazy? Have you looked around you? And what's this thing with you and Hudson? Are you working for him now? He hires only the best and you—"

"I can be the best," I say with a sniff, forgetting everything for a moment. Then I shake him off and breathe in. "It's temporary."

"And you didn't tell me." He steps in close. "What's really going on, Scarlett? Don't tell me you sold your soul to him. Or did something dumb."

I'm not too sure on the first one. Okay, I'm not too sure on both of those. "I can't talk to you here."

"Scarlett. Don't mess with him. He might come across as nice, but he's ruthless. And if this is about me, then don't."

"Look, we'll talk later, okay?" Hudson is approaching, I can feel it in the prickle of awareness down along my spine and I give Danny a not-so-gentle push. "I promise."

He stares at me a moment. "Okay."

Danny starts to lean in to kiss my cheek and I jerk away. He frowns.

"Later."

And then I spin around and nearly run into a blazing Hudson.

I wrap my hands around his forearms, find a smile and say, "Ready?"

I'm not an idiot. I don't think I've gotten away with anything, but I'm hoping, anyway.

We're outside in the night air and the people outside have to step out of his way or get run down by a billionaire god as we get in the back of his beautiful town car with the buttery leather seats that make me wish the car was mine.

Which is stupid. I'm a terrible driver and Manhattan terrified me the one and only time I drove through it.

He's silent and I'm almost about to congratulate myself on a pretty good dance when he speaks.

"I don't like being disobeyed, Scarlett."

"Is this why you're single?" The words came of their own accord and I slap a hand over my mouth.

He taps his hand on his thigh. "I'm single because relationships are messy and demanding in the wrong way, and I don't have time for them. I have sex, I fuck. I move on when I'm bored. I have understandings. And yes, I expect the lady in question to let me know if she's seeing someone else or going to be late."

I frown, dropping my hand. "That's not what I asked. I'm talking about giving orders and expecting them to follow."

"I'm not sleeping with you. I'm not dating you. I'm not even actually going to marry you. You are, for all intents and purposes, my employee. You're doing this for money. Because you need it and I'm doing it because you fit the services I require. So yes, in that instance I expect you to obey me."

He glares out the window.

I shiver. He's mad because I spoke to my brother…who he doesn't know is my brother. It doesn't make sense.

Oh, I'm lying, it does, because this is an arrangement between us and I'm in too deep to tell him the truth. And so I tango once again.

"I understand," I say as soothingly as I can, my mind ticking fast. I cross my legs and place my hand on his arm. "He came up and I sorted it out. That's all. I'm not *interested* in him."

And for once, it was the truth.

"I don't care—"

"Hudson," I cut in, "you have to trust me. I don't want you worrying about it."

"Scarlett—"

"Also," I drop in quickly because boy oh boy the softness in his voice worries me. Or something. It sends little shivers through me. "Also, I'm not going to let anything get in the way of you and your goals. That's what you employed me for."

He turns, his leg brushing mine as he does so, and he takes me in, but doesn't speak.

And I need to fill the void. Keep him in the dark from the actual truth. Keep him occupied in a sense of well-being and where he's not going to ask too many questions. I'm not sure how I'll do that, but I'm going to work on it. Anyway, I keep going.

"I take the job very seriously. After all, do well enough and there might be a bonus in it." I laugh and it's got a slight tinge of hysteria about it.

But he raises a brow, and the corner of his mouth rises in the kind of almost smile that sets blood pressure to emergency room levels. "Quite the little mercenary."

"Incentives work."

"So they do. And I really don't care who you talk to, just not on my watch. It doesn't sit well and if someone's watching they'll know I won't stand for it."

"We all have pasts."

His gaze moves over me again, this time slowly, and I'm possibly on fire. "And what's yours?"

A danger zone when it comes to this man.

"Boring. Rich girl stuff."

He laughs and shakes his head. "It's more than that, Scarlett. The job isn't Mayflower Matrons of the Hamptons or whatever it was. It's not tea parties and party dresses and Sunday brunches with the rich. It's work. But there can be some incentives…"

I swallow, because I don't know what he means. Or maybe I do. Or think I do. There's a light in his gaze, a predatory light that's way more single malt than martini and just as dangerous.

"Like what?"

He smiles, and it's a small smile. One that makes things dance and party in my stomach, that makes my blood heat in my veins. "I think maybe you should go before you find out."

"Well, now I want to know."

"Heard of what happened to the cat with curiosity?"

I slide my hand down his arm, knowing this is really stupid, but doing it anyway.

"Satisfaction, I imagine."

Hudson stares at me. "Are you insinuating that it was one very satisfied—" He stops himself and I can see the silent war there in his handsome face.

Anyone else he'd have said the word that hangs between us and its meanings. Anyone else he'd up that flirt and see what happened. Or take matters into his hands.

But it's me, or who he thinks is me, and he's being very careful.

I've had too many drinks, I decide, ignoring the fact I had maybe three. And that's the only reason I move my hand to his warm thigh, the muscle lean and hard beneath my fingers.

"Yes, that's what I'm saying."

His gaze is lingering on my mouth and then he shakes his head. "You need to behave, Scarlett. I don't want to complicate things. I'll walk you in."

And he gets out of the car.

We've stopped. I mean, he's not getting out of a moving car, is he? But I didn't notice, I was too wrapped up in him.

Putting my fingers on the door handle, it swings open before I can do anything and Hudson is there, helping me out. We're at Sarah's building, but I barely notice it because my blood is still hot in my veins and that wild party in my stomach has only gotten wilder.

"Goodnight," I say and then I grab him by the tie, draw him into me and kiss him.

It's better than I remember.

The kiss is brief. A taste of what could be. And his mouth tastes like Hudson—a mix of dark heat and promises that lie beneath the surface, and the sweet peat and malt of the Scotch.

His mouth is slightly open because I think he was going to speak, and he lets me taste him, a passive partner in whatever this is.

I go to break away. A different sort of heat that makes me want to slink away comes over me. But he doesn't let me. One of his arms comes around me like a steel band, and he whirls me so I'm pressed against the smooth metal of the car and the heat and need of him.

His eyes glitter as he looks down at me, a predatory light, and it strikes me he let me explore. The passiveness not a rejection, but an invitation to see what it was I wanted.

I don't know what I want.

Only I want more.

"If you're going to play with fire, Scarlett, you'll definitely get consumed by it."

I swallow. "A goodnight kiss—"

"Is not what that was. That felt like an invitation. If you don't want me to take it up, then let me know now."

There's a warning there and I can feel it, even as a reckless need pushes it aside. My fingers are still on his tie, making it pouf out from the waistcoat. It should look like he can't dress himself. It doesn't. It makes him look like a man who's having an extremely good time.

"I thought if someone is watching, we should put on a show."

He shifts, one of his legs sliding between my thighs, pushing lightly against my panties, against the heat and dampness that's there from this. Him. "A show?"

"Yes."

"For someone who might be watching?"

"Ye-e-ess..." The word hisses and hitches from me as he traces the shape of my lips with the finger of his free hand and I'm about to lose it.

I want to rub against his thigh. I want to get myself off on him. Lose myself in him.

His mouth lowers against my ear and his tongue draws patterns on my lobe, then traces my ear and I almost come from the little erotic thrills it rocks through me. "Like who?"

"Hypothetical someones. Spies?"

"Spies?"

His fingers dip down along my throat and tease the modest neckline of my dress. I'm shivering and I might be grinding against his leg. "Yesss."

"Well, let's give these hypothetical spies something to spy on. Don't want them losing jobs."

And before I can speak, he kisses me, soft, beguiling, the kind of kiss that draws me up and into him, makes me wrap my arms about him and press against the hardness of his body. It's seduction with a dark edge, and as he slides his tongue into my mouth, it morphs into something more and every single part of me is alive and throbbing with need.

If I could, I'd do him right here.

The kiss changes again and I'm a willing participant. This is the kind of dance where each touch and slide and step is prelude to sex, better than most sex I've ever had. It's a wild ride of hard and soft; aggression and gentle exploration; of absolute pleasure that has the promise of more.

And then it's over.

My head is spinning as he steps away like nothing happened.

Hudson smooths his tie back in place, and his gaze is so dark I could fall into it and be lost forever.

"For the spies. Goodnight."

I stand and watch him get in his car and drive away.

This isn't for show or to stall going into the building I don't live in. It's because I'm almost hyperventilating. Little rivers of desire and excitement are sparking and flaring into life all over me, and I'm not sure my feet work. I'm not sure I can breathe. I'm not sure I can get on the subway without being arrested for looking like I just had hot and dirty sex.

Can you get arrested for that?

I lied to him. I lied about the show. I lied to me. He might have done it to teach me some kind of lesson, or because he was bored, or maybe he thought a show might be a good idea.

But I did it because I like kissing him.

I like kissing him more than I've ever liked kissing anyone.

I might be in very big trouble.

Because even if he liked me back—which I doubt, but if he did—then there's nothing for us but a dead end. One of my own making.

One out of the very thing he crushes people like me over.

Lies.

Chapter Eleven

HUDSON

Over the next few days, I keep things strictly professional.

I have to, anyway, I have a tricky deal I'm pulling off and Scarlett needs to be able to keep up with my schedule and anticipate my needs.

She has a way of working that's intriguing, unusual, and it works. She calms people by talking and then charming them into forgetting whatever thing it was they wanted from me, and she's actually good at organizing things for me better than I would have, which is saying something. It's not the way I go about things, but it's logical in its own way and I'm not messing with it. Or her.

I'm definitely not messing with her.

Shit. That kiss... I'd only meant to warn her off or tease her and I hadn't expected it to be so mind blowing.

I don't like using that term, but it fits.

Turning my chair, I stare out the window at the deep blue sky from my office. The sun streams in like there are no cares in the world. But that's a stupid thought and I dismiss it.

What I can't dismiss is Scarlett and that scent; Scarlett and the dark honey hair and hazel eyes; Scarlett and those soft lips and hot kisses. What's worse is I can't dismiss her smart-ass mouth and surprising intelligence.

It's not surprising she's smart. I knew that when I first met her. What's surprising is the way her intelligence works, like she's plugged in a little differently.

It's alluring.

And fuck. I like her and I have to stop.

She has secrets, though, and I can't decide if they're ones everyone tends to have, or if they're big and going to fuck me over.

"Mr. Sinclair?" I look up, startled at Georgina.

She hovers nervously. You'd think the woman hadn't been working at my personal reception desk for the past eight years. "I knocked, but—"

"Sorry, lost in work." I look at her. And wait.

"Mr. Jenson is here."

"Send him in."

My father's lawyer walks in a few minutes later. He's an older man, and dressed expensively and conservatively, the way a rich man like my father would want his personal attorney to be. Subtle class that never overshadows.

He doesn't sit. Instead, Jenson wanders over to the floor to ceiling glass wall and puts his hands, linked, behind his back and stares out, the picture of ease.

I narrow my eyes.

And wait.

"Just wanted to drop by, see how things are going," Jenson says.

Crossing my legs, I nod. "You've never dropped by in your life. I doubt you've done that to your husband."

Jenson turns and shrugs. "Your mother also spoke to me, not long after you did. Between us, I don't give a fuck about the sincerity of this relationship, just that you pass the criteria. But your mother had questions."

Why my mother is in contact with my father's personal lawyer is anyone's guess. Then again, her relationship with my father after the divorce and all his subsequent divorces is also anyone's guess, so I leave it be.

"What sort of questions?"

Jenson shrugs again. "Who she is, and everything else. Your mother said she met her. She liked her, but she was...concerned about you getting involved with someone who works for you."

"It happens, and my money's more than protected. The family name, too." I lean back in my chair. "If that's her concern."

"Not everything is to do with the Sinclair name and money, Hudson."

I just laugh. He's so wrong.

"And it would be a union that must last past the cut-off date, as you well know," he says, delicately as possible. "As we discussed."

"Your concern and my mother's is...touching. But I'm old enough to take care of things on my own. I've gotten to this point in life, after all."

"I think—" Jenson starts to look uncomfortable at this point, "—your mother is concerned over your happiness."

"I have everything I want."

The man nods, then he comes up to my desk and the delicate veneer falls away. "You have less than four weeks to get everything you say you want, Hudson. Don't screw it up. It's the one and only chance."

"I'm aware." I make a point of looking at my watch. Scarlett will be here shortly with what I need before I head to my meeting, and this little get together has outstayed its welcome. "If there's anything more?"

"No, Hudson. Just remember what I said. And your mother's concerns."

"You're distracted."

I glance at Scarlett, who sits prim and proper and businesslike to the point of military issue armory, and I sigh.

She's bubbling beneath the surface. Too much energy that creeps into my blood, heightening my senses, and makes me too aware of her and way too aware of the tension between us.

"We've got less than four weeks now. It's time to up the ante."

She breathes out, running her hands over the thighs of her cropped trousers as she sits on the leather sofa in my office, looking for all the world like I've sentenced her to death. I frown.

But I don't say anything. I tuck it away as we get to work, finding myself distracted by her.

Scarlett smells too good, and I never realized before that subtle is a lot more dangerous than overt.

Subtle means I want to move closer, slide my mouth close to the skin of her throat as we go over the dates and what I need for work. It means I want to touch her, see if the top she wears, a lightly billowy thing in red that's buttoned up and casts shadows when the light is right and suggests if I get up close and real personal I might be able to see what lies beneath.

As we work, I hand her a printed page and our hands brush. It's an accident and it's like someone punched me in the solar plexus.

"I need those people," I say, pointing to the top four on the page. "I need them pushed back, but I need them not to feel like that."

She turns and hooks her hair behind her ear where she wears tiny little white gold studs I hadn't noticed before. Scarlett bites down on the corner of her lip and I want to lick it.

I'm not sure why I'm reacting this way. Maybe the kiss. Or maybe it's because I haven't had sex since before we met, which is odd because I had time last night, at drinks with my brothers and some woman who made it more than obvious she wanted me. Except I went home. Alone. My excuse was work, but truth is, that woman who has everything I like didn't do it for me.

"I could reschedule," Scarlett says, the soft slide of the material covering her thighs moves through me like music, "but from your face you don't want that."

If I continue to sit here so close to her I'm going to lose all sense of purpose. I get up and go to my desk where my phone is, and I quickly pull up my schedules for the next two weeks.

"It's not that. I just don't need them yet."

"I can butter them up. Send them little things—"

"I'm not a gift shop."

"What I mean is things that mean something to them. I'll talk to their people and keep them chugging along, like...like someone you think you'll want to date down the track but not now and you want to keep hanging on, for when you decide you want them."

Surprisingly apt, but I keep that thought to myself. "Like deep freeze?"

"But more pleasant." She grins and it lights up the room. "I'll get on to that for you."

My phone buzzes and it's Magnus.

Short and to the point.

Family bullshit thing. Be there. Tomorrow. The usual.

That's his way of saying there's a Sinclair family event that I've gone and forgotten about. Sure enough, it's there on my calendar. I text him back.

Wouldn't dream of it, I say.

Bring your project.

My brothers are all assholes. Jesus.

It doesn't matter. This could all be classed as a project, the thing with Scarlett, because in a way it is, I simply don't like it being called that.

I turn back to Scarlett, who's waiting for me, a little impatiently—not how a PA should be waiting, but I let it slide—and say, "I have a family event tomorrow. You're coming with me."

"It's Thursday."

The guy, Danny, her whatever the fuck he is, comes to mind and I give her a dark look as that thing I think might be jealousy stalks through me.

"Yes, it is." I move up to her, a little too close, and the heat between us rises and the pulse in her throat is leaping. "Problem?"

"No. I just...." She stops, then takes a breath, her hazel eyes deepening to topaz. "It doesn't matter."

"Out with it, Scarlett," I murmur, taking hold of her shoulders and drawing her closer. "We need to communicate or this won't work."

"Fine." Her voice is a little shaky, and her gaze drops to my mouth for a long beat I feel in my cock, and then back up to my eyes. "Fine. You tell me we have to keep things on the down low. But I'm your assistant, your PA, and you treated me like that the other night. So is this work or a date?"

"A date."

I didn't mean to say that, but the words are out.

"Well, how do we do that? So people believe it's natural. This is family—"

"I'll show you exactly how and why they'll believe this has progressed."

And I kiss her. It's seduction, pure and simple. Controlled, though it's hard, much harder than I thought it would be to do that, something I've never had a problem with before, and a work of art in its bringing her crumbling down around me.

Which she does.

Scarlett opens like night jasmine at the touch of the moon. She flowers for me, her mouth opening and inviting me in, the soft little sounds she makes as she kisses me back, the way her body flows in against me and I'm losing my footing, too.

It would be so easy to sink down into this, succumb to this creation of ours, and see where it leads.

But I don't.

I break the kiss.

Then I let her go and step back. "Like that, Scarlett."

She nods, her hand shaking as she raises it to her lips.

"You also need to make it look good," I say. "Now I have a meeting to get to."

"Ten-four, boss man," she said, but she's shaking when she leaves, which pleases me.

Her off kilter adds to the authenticity of what I'm attempting to pull off.

Problem is, I'm tangled up in this, too. Far more than I want, deeper than I should be.

And that doesn't please me at all.

Chapter Twelve

SCARLETT

There's panicking. And then there's this. Doomsday clock level of panic and the clock's about to set off Armageddon.

I'm exaggerating.

But I'm most definitely in a complete panic that threatens to swallow me whole.

It's Thursday night and I'm lost.

This is his family.

I didn't sign up for this.

And that kiss...on top of the other kisses... I didn't sign up for those, either. While they were glorious, what the hell is going to happen if it goes places?

Because if I'm honest with myself, he'd be able to seduce me with a look. I'm basically ready to rip off my panties for him. That's not exactly the proudest moment of my life, that admission, but it's true.

If that happens, I'm going to have to magically get him to his place. Considering our kisses—apart from his lesson at the office—happen outside my not address, I might have to bring him back here.

I shove my icy fingers against my hot face.

What am I thinking? We're not going to have sex.

I'm living in a fantasy world.

Yes, but I also never thought he'd kiss me and I have to girl scout it. Be ready. Earn a badge.

If something happens, I'm in trouble.

Also, I need an outfit.

"Amber!" I race from my room and into hers, where she's lounging on her bed reading a book. "I need help."

"Girl, I could have told you that." She stops, sitting up. "What do you mean help?"

I can't tell her the truth. There's an NDA. There's the threat that Hudson made.

It's all very real.

I'm going to have to cram more small lies in.

"Clothes and... There's a man."

Her squeal of joy stabs at me for the lie. Okay, there is a man, but it's not what she thinks. Still, I quickly pick and choose my words, keeping it vague and with just enough information to keep her satisfied for now. I hope. "He has money and he seems nice."

Even I know that's lame.

There are a lot of words out there to describe Hudson, but nice is definitely not one of them. A sugar cookie is nice; a sunny, warm day is nice. Hudson is an exquisite martini in a dark, decadent speakeasy.

"Go you, nabbing a rich, mysterious dude, Scarlett." She's on her feet and digging about in her closet. "What's his name?"

Terror grips me, which is completely stupid. I'm a grown woman.

"What I need is a plan and a dress."

Amber spins to face me, hands on her hips. Her eyes narrow. "Do not tell me he's married."

"No!" I cross my heart with my finger. "I'm not that stupid."

Clearly, I'm some kind of stupid, but not that.

"So why—"

"It's really new and I don't know if this is in my head or if there's something else, but he asked me to go to this thing and..." I drop my voice even though we're in her bedroom, "I work with him."

Her eyes widen. "Why didn't you just say, 'hey, Amber, I gots me a maybe thing with a rich, hot dude I'm working with'?"

"I thought I did."

"No, you did not, Scarlett. You did not. Office romances are hot AF, but also frowned upon, and if he's rich, then you're not on the same pay level, so there's an imbalance of power—also frowned upon and also hot as fuck. So, let me find you a dress and then we have to go shopping this weekend."

My head is spinning. I have no idea where she got the whole office dynamic thing from, but I dismiss it. There's too much going on and she's right, it is hot AF. "Shopping?"

"Yes, that thing you do to buy things."

"I shouldn't spend money."

I still need to help my brother, and I haven't passed the test yet to get Hudson what he wants, and that means I haven't been paid.

Amber rolled her eyes. "Spending money is your god given right as an American. And it's fun. You're going to need some outfits and there are some good places we can go that are affordable."

"Okay. But help me tonight, first."

"Deal."

An hour later, I'm waiting outside the apartment building. I actually got here early enough I chatted with the doorman, and buttered him up with some cookies from the best little bakery near my subway stop.

Not only did Amber pick the dress tonight from her collection, she helped me with a plan in case something happens with Hudson. Which it won't. But...just in case, we've decided to say that I had to stay with my friend out in Brooklyn due to an issue in my apartment.

He's not going to buy that, but it's worth a shot, and besides Sarah's the type to pretend she has more money than she does.

The difference is she actually comes from money and I don't.

Hudson's car pulls up and he gets out in a dark suit that makes my mouth water. It's not black, it's richer than black, but I can't say what color it is, exactly, only that it makes him sexy and dangerous and debonair.

He comes to a stop, his gaze moving over me. It's possessive and it sends a thrill through my flesh.

"I like the color."

The wine red of the simple silky shift suits me, and the dress looks quality without trying. I don't own much jewelry, so I'm wearing my studs in my ears and a simple white gold slender bracelet with a little four-leaf clover on it that is the only thing I have of my grandmother.

"Thank you."

He leads me to the car and the tension and awareness is thick and tight between us as we cut across Manhattan to the Upper East Side to East Seventy-Ninth Street and a beautiful old apartment building with the old servant quarters on the roof.

Hudson obviously knows the place as we waltz in and take an elevator that skips the first twenty floors until we come to the top floor. It opens into a vast room of glamor and money and taste.

We say hello to people, or he does, and then Hudson leads me outside to the wrap-around rooftop that's more like a deck than anything else. It's beautifully landscaped and we finally come to stop, taking in the view.

At least I am, because when I turn, he's looking at me.

My mouth goes dry.

"A breath of fresh air and the stunning view before family time."

I gloss over the view part of his sentence because it doesn't mean what my head's suddenly thrown at me and I get myself ready. "What's the plan?"

"Look good, stay with me, and act like you're into me."

"I'm a good actress," I say airily. "I should be able to pull that off."

A low smile hits his mouth. "No one will ever see the struggles."

"God, no."

The evening spins out and his mother is the perfect hostess for what's clearly a fundraiser for a school for the underprivileged. His brothers come over to chat, but they're all checking me out. And through it, Hudson is a dream.

Attentive, always there, smiling, little touches that border on intimate, and inside hope begins to form. Insane hope, obviously, because I'm not even sure what I'm hoping for except that I'm attracted to him and I think he likes me, too. At least enough to sleep with me.

I don't go around sleeping with people just because they're hot, or they want to get their rocks off with me. But the crazy part inside is willing to go for it, no matter what my brain might say. And my brain isn't saying much, as I think it's drunk on desire.

Somewhere a quiet little voice says this is what he wants. Me feeling like this is real. But I squash that voice.

The tension between us grows thick, intense, and it crackles in the air and sends heat cascading through me every time he looks at me. And finally, Hudson leans over and says, "Want to get out of here?"

I nod, and I'm not above having fantasies of him having his wicked way with me in the elevator down. He doesn't and the matronly woman sharing the ride might have something to do with it.

The night is warm and lovely when we get down to the street, and his car pulls up like magic.

The ride to my—Sarah's—building is short and long and weird and full of anticipation of what's going to happen next.

He gets out of the car and opens my door and helps me out, and then I turn to him and wait because I'm not going to be the one to kiss him. He leans in. My eyelids flutter shut.

"Goodnight, Scarlett."

And he's gone.

I stare after him.

What the hell was that?

Last night I tossed and turned and it took forever to get to sleep.

It's not like I haven't been rejected. I've been rejected. A lot. But I didn't expect...that.

The tension had built so high and tight it was at breaking point and I was primed and ready and he just disappeared.

And to top it off, I got to work early this morning and I haven't seen him at all, and it's late in the afternoon now.

All my self-righteous indignation has fizzled into mortification and that's just turned itself into disappointment laced with confusion.

Maybe I got everything wrong.

I draw in a breath and stare at the email I'm writing on the computer and pay it zero attention. At least this means I can get out of here and meet up with my brother like I promised him. I owe him about a million explanations, and I have exactly nothing but tiny lies to offer and that really sucks.

Suddenly my skin pricks all over and a shiver of heat passes through me, and I know without turning that Hudson is there.

"My office."

I get up and follow and shut the door behind me. "Yes?"

"Sorry, I had meetings all day."

My heart starts to pick up its pace and beat hard and fast in my chest.

His gaze meets mine and everything is magma hot. "Stay late."

"I can do that."

He picks up his tablet, leans against his desk, and doesn't look at me. "I wasn't aware that was a multiple choice. Or a question."

A different kind of heat, miserable and dark, swamps me. "Oh."

"I've got more meetings and I have a big deal, last minute, that's tricky and I need help."

My eyes blur for some stupid, idiotic reason. They're hot, too. And there's a lump the size of this building in my throat. I stare down at the darkly polished floorboards. "That's what I'm here for. Your PA. Employee. In every aspect of your life."

I don't mean those last words, but they come out. I sound petulant and bitter and maybe it's because I am right now. Damn it.

"Is something wrong, Scarlett?" he asks, sounding totally bored.

"No. Why?"

"Oh, I don't know." The sarcasm is there now and it hurts. "I was just talking and you ignored me. And, hmmm, let me think? Oh, yes. That other thing you said in that tone."

"I don't know what you're talking about."

"Don't you?" He straightens and comes to me, and I've blinked away enough tears to look at him and I sort of wish I hadn't, because he's breath stealing kind of gorgeous. And I think I hate him. "I remember a few minutes ago when you said you're just an employee in all aspects of my life."

"Well, aren't I?"

"Did you think you're not?"

I grit my teeth to stop myself saying things, mean things, bad things, regretful things.

"Scarlett?"

"I'm not sure what to think, after—" I snap my mouth shut.

And he just looks at me. "After what? The kiss in my office? Paying you attention last night?"

I glare at him.

"The first was to prove a point and the second was part of the setup."

I don't answer.

"Why, Scarlett, you didn't think this was for real," he says, "did you?"

I hate him.

Chapter Thirteen

HUDSON

I'm being mean to her.

The thought trickles into my brain about an hour into our work.

Or, should I say, was.

Since I taunted her, it's been work and pure business politeness, which from the way the smile's gone and the light's dimmed in her, says it might be worse.

My office is spacious, the kind of spacious it could be carved into a three-bedroom apartment. Yet it feels small.

The last of the day's sunlight is streaming, giving the place a buoyancy that doesn't feel that way. No, it feels dark and oppressive, and like I need to get the fuck out and get some fresh air.

Scarlett's also mad.

Not a tantrum throwing, look at me anger, but something deeper, more real, and that circles back to hurt.

I'm not a cruel person, at least, I don't go out of my way to do so. That doesn't get me the results I want in business. Obviously, I'm no pushover but the fact she's hurting is...

Leaning back in the armchair angled next to the sofa, I think about it as I lock my fingers together over my abs.

I really have no idea why I said that. But there's something, deep down, that says differently. It's her. Everything about her and the ways she surprises me; her scent, her mind, that mouth.

There's no way around it. I'm way too attracted to her.

Fuck.

I push up and go to the wet bar and pour a drink. I need the boost. Or the edge taken off, and it's going to be a long night for me. Then I pour one for her and take it over.

"No, thank you."

"Take it," I snarl.

Her eyes narrow. "You made your point, sir."

"Just take it." I soften my voice and continue to hold it out. "Please."

"What is it?"

"Dirty martini, rocks."

Her mouth sets and for a moment I don't think she's going to take it, but she finally wraps her fingers around the low ball and they brush against mine, sending cascades of shivery sparks of need through me. All the way down. To my cock.

And just like that, I switch gears.

Just because I'm urbane doesn't mean I don't know how to hunt with skill and deadly determination.

I haven't decided how far to go because the situation is delicate.

But she's there.

So am I.

And the want beats hard between us.

That whispery kiss of her fingers against mine tells me that. The looks she gives when she doesn't think I'm paying attention. But I am. Always. This time when we resume work, I sit closer to her, on the sofa, and the heat rises.

Little touches linger. Words are softer, sweet murmurs subconsciously designed to draw me closer to her, bend my head a little nearer.

And I'm half erect. A thrill is in my blood. I don't think there's been a woman I've wanted like I do her. It could be the forbidden element—what there is of one, the job at hand; and it could be the ease—what there is, the job at hand. But it doesn't matter. She's there, and so am I.

Sliding my hand along the back of the sofa, I lean in to see what she's talking about, the juggling of intricate things I need done right, and my fingers thread through her hair and she turns, her words dying as her breath stutters.

My gaze drops to her mouth.

"Hudson..."

I want to kiss her again. The need and urge are real.

Moving a little closer, I feather my lips along hers and she sighs. "This what you want, Scarlett?"

"You're an ass," she whispers as she leans into me, turning her head just so, and her soft, sweet tasting lips are there for the taking, and I do.

It's a nothing kiss, the kind that's made of dreams, but under that delicate surface beats the blood and bones of the attraction. The erotic edge, and I want to take it further, slide down deep into her, and strip her naked as I slide on home.

"Yeah," I say, breaking that kiss, "I am. I've been thinking of exactly what we're doing here."

"Work?"

I laugh and shake my head and get to my feet. The predator moves inside me and the game is subtle and full of the right kind of waiting.

"Something like that, Scarlett."

She scowls, pushing up to her feet and stomping to me, poking me in the chest in the way no one ever dares to unless they happen to be one of my brothers or someone with a death wish.

"Don't do that."

Anyone else I'd do something about it. But I want to see where she's going and I'm not going to lie, the passion of her low-down anger riles me in all the right ways, including my curiosity. So I let her poke. For now.

"Do what? You're the one doing, Scarlett."

Her scowl deepens and she pokes harder. It strikes me she'd be fucking hot to do right now, but I keep that on a controlled backburn. "I'm not doing anything."

"You're poking me."

"Because you deserve to be beaten up and I can't do that."

"Too afraid?"

"Yes. And I'm not strong enough." She breathes out hard. "You keep kissing me and then toying with me and getting angry at me if I speak to someone of the male persuasion. And then you go and tell me we can't tell anyone."

"To be fair, you want me to kiss you."

"So? That's not an answer." Scarlett motors onward, her admission not slowing anything down. "You have it, so I don't know which foot to put forward and that's not fair."

I'm not being fair. I know it. I capture her hand and hold it against my chest, rubbing my thumb over her fingers. "We're playing a game, Scarlett. Part of that is mimicking what they call love." The word tastes bitter.

"You don't believe in love."

I sigh. "And you believe in all the fairy tales of the Disney variety, don't you?"

"Would that be a bad thing?"

"It's make believe."

"Again, why would that be a bad thing? I know what this is, even if you hadn't gone out of your way to point it out. Even if we got down and dirty together, I wouldn't mistake it as love. It's, as you put it, a game."

I look at her.

She's either playing it perfectly or she's telling me the truth. "Women have a habit of falling in love to get what they want, and men have a habit of pretending to get what they want."

"Who hurt you?"

I almost let her go, but don't. Mainly because I like the heat and the feel of her in my hand, I like her so close. I like that tease of flowers in the air.

"No one," I say.

And it's true. I don't have relationships, just sex, and carefully curated affairs that mimic short-term relationships. You could, I suppose, argue those affairs are relationships, but they're sex. Sex and compatibility for when I need to step out in the world with whoever the woman is by my side.

I guess that's what this is. Without the sex. And I'm creating, not curating.

The no sex thing is not written in stone, no matter how dangerous sex with Scarlett might be.

"Everyone gets hurt."

"Then everyone's an idiot." I continue to draw patterns on her hand. "My life is work and things contained in neat boxes for efficiency."

"That's sad," she says, her voice soft.

I raise a brow. "That's being smart."

"So kissing me is smart?"

"No," I say, brushing her mouth with mine, "that's stupid and messy."

"And you like it."

"Yes."

She's quiet a long time, while the soft hum of awareness and attraction fills the air around us. "How are you going to pull off being in love if you don't believe in it?"

That's a good question. "We get to know each other like I said and—"

"Act?" She shakes her head. "You're working to get me confused and mimic love, but you actively push it away. The idea, I mean."

"I'm paying you, Scarlett, not the other way around. I didn't get to where I am—family money aside—without determination and brains. I've got this. Just make sure you do, too."

"Was it your parents?"

"Excuse me?"

"Who hurt you." She's not letting it go.

And I sigh. "Yes and no. Yes, my parents split up and my mother built her own life too close to my father's. He kept marrying younger versions of her, and she'd be there to pick up the pieces after each one. I don't know what they were doing, but it was counterproductive and messy and something I've no interest in. But no, that didn't hurt me, just showed me how things don't work in life. That's all."

Abruptly, I let her go. "Hungry?"

"Excuse me?"

"Food. That stuff you put in your mouth for fuel. I'm hungry. We've got more work to do because you're going to be eyebrow deep in everything this week in regards to work and I can't check over things, so measure twice, right?"

"I'll get my extra big pair of scissors." She rubs a hand over her face and then steps back from me, turning and going to sit down again. "Yes. Food would be good. Thank you."

I ordered Omani food. There's a new place that was opened by a chef who lived in Oman and wanted to bring the unknown dishes of the area to the West. This is what Ryder told me, anyway. Anything to do with indulging the senses and I'll take his word for it. Except for women. He's got a problem there.

The contemplative expression on Scarlett's face as she finished her Kabsa, an aromatic saffron rice dish with red spiced chicken, was a delight. As is the sweet bliss that blossoms when she finishes the ice cream I also ordered.

I've never found someone else enjoying their food erotic, until now. But with her, that enjoyment is definitely erotic, and it only makes me wonder what else she savors, and how she'd bring that to bed. Or wherever fucking her might take place.

Work is done and I'm finding things to do, which I can't stop myself from doing. Yes, I need to go over things because that's how I am, but I know it's her.

She keeps me lingering. Making me keep her lingering.

I have another drink. Too much and I might cross lines I'm not yet willing to cross. She makes that hard without alcohol. But I feel good, there's a latent lethargy spreading through me, belying the coiled predator within.

"That was all…amazing."

I glance at her. "Said like a woman who's only eaten at the in places."

"Yes, well." Her small smile slips and a darkness shadows her eyes as she glances away. But when she looks back it's gone. "Maybe you don't know me as well as you think."

"I don't know you," I say, even though I'm beginning to, and I do in a lot of surprising ways, but that's not what she means. "That's the point of all this."

She shuts down the iPad and sets it on the coffee table. I admire the way her top stretches just a little to show her form beneath. "I think we're done for the night."

"Are we?"

Her gaze skitters over to me and her cheeks turn pink. She swallows. "I didn't mean—"

"You did, you know," I say, setting down my glass and leaning in toward her. "You have a habit of overstepping all kinds of boundaries. That doesn't make you the best well-bred society girl out there."

"And what does it make me?" she snaps.

"Interesting."

The word sits, and with it, the tension rises and I slide my hand up over her cheek, her skin impossibly soft and warm. "Oh."

"There you go again. You accuse me of back and forth and here you are, doing it yourself. Your Scarlett brand. You're nothing like any of the women I've met from your world."

"Is that a compliment?"

I smile. "Take it as you wish."

Christ, I want her mouth again. It's calling to me and I'm not strapped to any mast at all. Kiss her again and I might not be able to help myself.

I trace along beneath her bottom lip with my thumb and I'm rewarded with her sharp little intake of breath and the lean into my hand and my touch. It's enough to give me a raging erection.

"Hudson..."

My name is a revelation from her lips. It's full of need and promises and longing and yeah, that does things to me, too. The way she says it.

"You really are different. I can't put my finger on it," I say, shifting a little closer to her, wanting to breathe her in again. "Bixby never really spoke about you." Bixby was by the book and still is. We're not close, but... I try to fit them together as a family and can't. Her side must be something to behold. Or else it's her. An outlier in that microcosm world. "Tell me about your family."

Everything changes.

Scarlett suddenly goes still, eyes wide. And she pulls back then, from my touch, jumping up to her feet.

"I think I've got the hang of it all. I mean, I do. And as you said, we have a busy week and lots to do on all fronts. I need an early night. I'll get a cab."

Without another world, she spins and races out the door.

And if I didn't know better, I'd swear she just ran away.

Chapter Fourteen

SCARLETT

I just ran away from Hudson.

Shit.

I shouldn't have done that, but I needed to.

I'm standing outside the elevator, panting out of fear rather than the run from his office, waiting for the damn elevator to turn up.

The smart lights came on with each step I took and the ones where I am light me like I'm some escapee caught in a spotlight.

Standing…panicking…shifting like a maniac from one foot to the other on the rich cream carpet that covers the floor, that's what I'm doing. It must cost a fortune to clean. Good thing he's a billionaire. I almost start laughing but swallow the hysteria down with my nonsensical thoughts. And I'm resisting the urge to look back over my shoulder.

He isn't coming. I'd know. I'd hear him and looking back makes me look every bit the crazy and guilty person I am.

I press the button again and again. But the elevator, which I know moves smooth and fast, has suddenly morphed into something super slow.

I should not have run from him when he asked that question, but what am I meant to say? That I told him a big, fat white lie that keeps bleeding bigger and bigger, not to mention sprouting new ones?

And what was that whole thing in his office where my internal temperature must have been hotter than the sun? The kiss? Those touches?

I'm not even claiming to be innocent because I took part fully. I wanted to touch him, and I did.

Apparently, I like playing with sexy fire.

Sexy fire that has influence with a capital I and bells, whistles, and parades in the same arena where my brother's struggling to find his foothold once again. A black strike or black ball or whatever term you want to use thrown against him means he's dead in the water, career wise. And Danny sank his money, my money, our grandparents' money, into it when he set out with a dream.

He aligned with the wrong person and now he's barely treading water—I don't know where the whole watery analogy thing comes from. It's probably because I'm in over my head and I feel like I'm drowning.

But my point is, Hudson, the man I'm attempting to run from and am thwarted by an elevator at the top of a Manhattan modern business castle, can make or break or squash people like Danny.

And I'm lying to Hudson.

Little spidery white lies that breed.

I'm lying and I'm crossing all the boundaries and I'm not sure if I've bitten off too much, if I can breathe under this water or deal with any of it.

But I have to. I need to keep calm and just keep going and glue all the pieces together. If I need to get gaffa tape to help, I'll do it.

Every little, tiny bit of research on Hudson I've done comes crashing back. Everything he's said. This man doesn't make threats, he's a martini so smooth you never realize the bite is real until you're at the bottom of the glass. And he doesn't make threats at all.

Hudson Sinclair makes promises.

He can destroy Danny.

These are things I know and have to keep front and center of my brain until I see this thing through to the end. I'm not in it to hurt anyone.

A dark shiver passes through me. It's like every part of me suddenly burst into a different kind of life.

"It doesn't come faster if you keep pushing the button."

It's not until Hudson speaks I realize I'm doing just that.

Those smooth, velvet tones are like whispering kisses against my skin.

"I'm in a hurry."

"To get home?"

I don't turn to face him. I can't. "Yes."

The elevator chooses that moment to whoosh smoothly open and to my horror and perverse delight, Hudson ushers me inside.

"You know," he says, "if you keep this up, running away, hiding your face, then it's not going to work."

I snap around to face him. "What isn't?"

He's like a sucker punch.

How do I keep forgetting how beautiful the man is?

"Pulling this whole thing off." He smiles, and it's small and genuine. Hudson leans against the other side of the elevator, facing me, his hands behind his back as he does so. "I've been thinking."

"It could be dangerous."

There's a spark of laughter in his gaze, and right there is why I have trouble with remembering the whole he can destroy me and my brother thing. The good guy part of him, the decent man. But just because he's that doesn't mean he'll unleash his wrath if you do him wrong.

I don't intend to. I just don't intend to tell him the small details.

"Look, I don't know a thing about your family. I know your cousin, but it's not a best friends thing. You get it."

"Our kind stick together against the great unwashed masses of the world." I don't even know why I say that. It just seems like something someone very rich would say. And though Sarah never said it, she's definitely looked down on the poor. Probably looked down on me at one point. And we're not besties, either, just friends.

An eyebrow quirks up. "That's one very snotty way to put it, I suppose. I just mean…"

"I know what you mean. Our world."

I don't know at all.

Now he frowns at me and he's looking at me in a way that makes me uncomfortable, like he can somehow see the truth inside. "No. I meant he's someone I knew a long time ago and kept in touch with over the years on a basic level. That's all."

He stops.

I can't breathe because he straightens up and comes to me and every atom in me wants him.

He slides his fingers through my hair and says softly, "Sometimes you're like two different people in there."

"I go to therapy." Against all commonsense, I bring my hand up and place it against the hard muscles that lurk beneath his suit. And I have the sudden urge to see him in jeans and a T.

"Why did you run, Scarlett?" His voice is pure, soft, decadent velvet and I'm melting into total pliability. "What deep, dark secrets are you hiding?"

Those words send such a bolt of fear through me that I stop melting immediately and get the gaffa tape to hold it together. "Nothing. Just...usual family crap."

"Well, I think we should talk."

The elevator swishes open and we're out in the beautiful, vast foyer of marble and steel and glass. The security guard nods to Hudson and then we're outside in the cooling night air, the sounds of New York and its never-ending traffic rising up around us.

I'm about to say goodnight when he slips his hand under my elbow.

"Hudson, I only had the one drink. I'm not drunk."

"I didn't think you were," he says, hailing a cab and scooting me over the pavement and onto it. "We need to talk."

Those words put the fear of fate worse than death into me, followed by a desire deeper than the Grand C because he meant a chat over a drink in a small little bar nestled in Greenwich Village.

Hudson in his suit in a bar of hipsters and simple jeans and T-shirt every day folk should have made him stand out like some kind of sore thumb.

It didn't.

At all.

Oh, he stood out, but in that way some spend years trying to achieve. The women kept stealing looks at him, men, too. And he didn't notice at all.

This is my kind of place. No pretention. Ratty barstools from years of use in a long, thin sliver of a bar.

But I'd never seen this place before. Hole in the wall would be the term along with neighborhood.

I give him a long look.

"Not your style?" He lifts his glass of dark amber liquid and takes a sip. There's a martini in front of me, and I take a small swallow and almost drop it. "I thought it would be right up your alley. How's your drink?"

Like fresh apples, smooth and a kick that's nestled all the way down the bottom. "Retro."

"Yes, well, they didn't have olive branches."

An appletini does not say olive branch to me. It says sly sense of humor hidden in the dark depths of the man opposite who grows more intriguing by the minute, and more forbidden apple than anything else.

He taps a hand against the bar where we sit, very close. It's not packed in here, but there are enough people that sitting close is a good idea. Or a bad one.

"I've been thinking, Scarlett."

"Should I be worried?"

"No, I do it all the time," he says, so deadpan I almost laugh. "I was thinking about everything you said, people knowing. I don't like lies, but we're telling one."

"A big one," I point out.

He gives me a strange look. "Yes, I know. But close to the truth is best. So we stick to our plan, get to know each other and if someone asks about us, then tell them our truth. As vague as you can."

"That's a lie."

"It's the same one."

"I tell them I'm doing this to help you out?" I don't know why I say that. I swallow. "That's a joke. What if it's media?"

"I'm rich, not famous. I'm not in any media unless it's financial or something equally boring. The occasional page whatever the fuck it is because I'm at an event I can't get out of."

"We've been over this."

"It's worth repeating."

Maybe. "But—"

"Scarlett. You talk a whole lot." His hand comes down over mine and it sends desire racing through me, prickling against my senses. "That's fine. I'm used to it now."

His smile takes any sting from his words.

"What I'm trying to say," he says, continuing, "is I want to be super prepared. Which is why I asked about your family tonight. No other reason."

Half of me breathes a sigh of relief and the other, more stupid part, is offended.

I have to keep reminding myself this is a job, nothing more.

"Oh," I say, "there's nothing really there. It's just...we're not close, you know?"

That's one way to put it. Another is I don't know much about Sarah's actual family because she never talked about them much, just her cousin. I know she's an only child, though. Anyway, less is definitely a whole lot more here.

I take a breath. "So, anyway, it's more about you and me and if we can convince the powers that be, so to speak, right?"

"Yeah."

I don't like how he says that.

"You don't look happy, Hudson."

"I want things I'll get if we pull this off and I can't shake the feeling someone's waiting for me to slip up."

"Or it's your guilty conscience."

If he wasn't basically holding my hand, I'd slap it over my mouth. I'm gripping the martini glass with the other, mid air, having decided moments ago to take a sip.

"I'm not feeling guilty. Just looking at all contingencies." Then he looks down and seems to realize he has his hand on mine. He pulls it away. "I thought we'd have a drink and relax, and I'd make sure things were good."

If there was a mood, he'd have killed it, right there.

I go to bed that night—we wrap up after that one drink because I was adamant my bungled running away was all about wanting an early night—pleased with myself, because my vagaries have worked.

It's not until morning my self-congratulations start to wobble, but I get out the glue and gaffa tape and bind it all together in one big ball of it's all going to be okayness.

I work hard during the day, I'm multitasking like I'm one of my AIs I'm training and I'm into some kind of groove with micromanaging Hudson's life.

His meetings run like clockwork and if there's a bit of behind the scenes fixing things, I do it.

At seven p.m. he texts to tell me to go home as he's holed up in a long-ass meeting with his brothers. And I'm feeling good, I'm feeling fine. The weather is nice and it's not too hot either.

Thanks for everything, Scarlett, Hudson suddenly texts me. ***I appreciate your honesty and you going the extra distance. I'm sometimes not the easiest man.***

Well...shit. My plan is working. My plan is I don't have one, other than get through this, but it's working. Go me.

Since it's really lovely out, I walk from midtown West to the East side and find myself on First Avenue and East Third. There's a cheap little bar and basic taco place that makes everything from scratch, so I stop there and eat.

There's something in the back of my head, something that scratches at my skin that makes me itch, but I ignore it. Hudson's probably seen the light or something and realized I'm brilliant. That's all. I'm not used to out of nowhere praise.

And I am being honest. Sort of. In a way. I mean, he's paying me to lie and all I've done is tell him a lie. Or ten.

It's all good.

I pull out a book and get a Coke and sit back down in my plastic seat at the taco place and read.

But around nine I'm still here in Manhattan and the guilt at what I'm doing, the lies, eats at me. I've wandered through Tompkins Square Park. I even read about the riot back in the nineteenth century that happened there, but I only half paid attention because my brain is tallying the lies and I'm swamped.

Stupid guilt. I hate it.

It's not until I'm walking uptown again, I realize where I'm going.

To Hudson's place.

He might not even be there. Who knows what he's up to with his brothers tonight. But I keep going.

I probably shouldn't have the address. But I do, I peeked in the files I've access to.

All these kisses and lies are just getting to me and if something happens between me and him, happens physically—the naked, hot, sweaty kind of physically—I need it to be a clean slate, honesty. Transparency like the cleanest, thinnest glass.

It's only really a small lie and it's best I come out and tell him now.

That's my plan.

It's why I'm heading to his place.

I'm going to tell him the truth before things get more complicated.

After all, how bad could it be?

Chapter Fifteen

HUDSON

"Hudson!"

Shock runs through me at the sight of Scarlett on my doorstep, the light from the door turning her hair into dark, shining honeyed fire.

I'm not sure why she sounds shocked. After all, I didn't invite her. I didn't even know she had my address.

"I live here."

I've had drinks with my brothers so I'm feeling a little looser, and things are good.

"So you do. I wanted—" Scarlett stops. She blinks and whatever she's going to say doesn't see light of day because she pivots. I can almost see it happening.

Her gaze slides down over me in my jeans and shirt.

"Yes?"

She looks up at me, those hazel eyes like honey and just as sweet lock on mine. "You're wearing jeans."

"It's been known. I don't live in a suit." Though sometimes it feels like it. I lean against the door and hook my thumbs in the back pockets of the jeans. "You're still wearing your work clothes."

"Yes, I am."

I realize I could stay here, all night, just poking at her gently, getting reactions, seeing what she'll say next. I also realize I could do a lot of things with her, if I let myself. "Was there a reason you rang my door? I'm not even asking how you got my address." She doesn't answer. "Or was it you just wanted to gaze at me?"

Color burns high and dark in her cheeks. "I am not." Her eyes narrow. "Gazing at you."

"You are, you know. Otherwise, it'd be rude."

I might be slightly veering toward the tipsy side of things, but I'm in control. It's just with her, control has a habit of slipping away at the best of times.

"So," I say, "why'd you come here?"

"Oh. Oh! I figured we could go out."

It's a terrible idea. And I like it. For once, I could actually go for some fun and I already know Scarlett can be a hell of a lot of fun.

It's not that I don't have fun with my brothers—Ryder, anyway. But tonight wasn't that. Tonight was business, this whole thing, right here with Scarlett and what it means to them. None of us have any idea. But it seems even Magnus is invested, for whatever darkly ruthless reasons he might have. Kingston, well, he's a cynic, but he's family and he's intrigued on whatever level it is. Ryder would love a real piece of our family history and he wants me to succeed so he can see the mysterious Sinclair jewels, no matter how laid back about it he pretends to be.

And Ryder also pieced together some things, too. Which makes the whole Sinclair jewels thing more important than ever for me.

Why they were hidden and steeped in rumor and legend is anyone's guess, since those who knew are all dead, but legacy is important. It's part of being a Sinclair. Part of my identity.

Ryder's on board with that. Magnus wants power and means, and Kingston, too, if it's worth anything to him, money-wise.

That wasn't the only reason we met up. Business is business after all and sometimes, since we're all in the world of real estate in different ways, our interests cross. We also met for a catch up, too.

And I've had just that little too much to drink to make me decide dangerous fun, Scarlett-style, is the way to go.

"Okay."

She blinks at me. "Okay?"

"Yes. Let's have some fun. Things today went well and you actually somehow managed to make tomorrow's load a lot easier. The rest of the week's actually. Good job." I stop. I don't want to talk about work. Not right now. "So yeah, let's have fun."

After all, it's not like I'm going to cross lines. Just perhaps dabble with them, push and nudge them. That is, if I feel like it. And she smells so unbelievably good.

"You want to have fun? I thought there was a law against it in Hudson Martini world."

I grab my phone, wallet, and keys from the side table just inside the door, pull it shut and lock it, and then I gesture to the wide world of Manhattan that's my doorstep. "No law. I'm not against fun, Scarlett. I just don't have much time or use for it in my life."

"That's sad."

Is it? I never missed it. But Scarlett has a way of getting into the blood and twisting things up. She's a game changer. And to me it's a revelation that her work clothes are chameleon, like her, something I'd never put together until now. She's not flashy, but she could fit in most places. She's got a mouth on her, but she's able to work with all kinds of situations, from how she handled people at my event, to having the guts to stand up to me.

It's there, she hides it, but it's there.

And I don't know why I'm thinking this at all, except it's like I'm seeing her all at once for the first time and a layer melted away.

But right now, I don't want to go there or put my head in the game. The light buzz in my veins ticks up when I grab her hand and lead her down to the street. I don't want that to go.

"Well, maybe you can do something about it, Scarlett."

She looks up at me and a smile breaks free. "Oh, no. That's like a get out of jail free card. Why don't you show me you can do something about it."

"Okay," I say, not letting go of her hand, "you're on."

The bar in Dumbo is popping, as they say, but it's some place I know as I own property here, near the waterfront amongst the cobblestoned streets and high-end stores and everything that makes it so sought after. The up-close view of the Manhattan bridge isn't bad, either.

"You're into Brooklyn?" Scarlett asks, leaning in close to be heard over the noise in the glass and industrial steel vibe bar with plants and swathes of artistically deconstructed white paint on the walls.

I shrug and take a swallow of my Scotch. "I'm not against it." I eye her again. It's an easy thing to do as we lounge on the bench in the corner.

She's good to be around, and that's been the deal the whole time, not some new thing. The revelation is more me than her. Me not fighting it. I don't like stepping into territory I haven't studied and dissected and weighed up.

That's what this whole thing is, my rash decision. Because for me it was rash. But if I let myself lean into it, then the natural attraction between us works.

It works in my favor, and I need it to work.

She fidgets with her drink. Gin this time, the purple stuff that changes to pink because of whatever flower is used. I don't really keep up with the latest trends like Ryder. I like it simple and quality because that's where depth and complexity and reward lie.

"So, about all this," she says, not looking up.

I glance about, deliberately obtuse. "The bar? Or Brooklyn?"

Her sharp glance makes me smile. Most people would hide that irritation under careful layers because they know who I am. Not Scarlett. What seemed rough edged and gave me doubts is the breath of everything I need and refreshing. "No."

"What about the contract?" A sliver of something cold and liquid runs down my spine. "You seem like you have something on your mind. Do you want out?"

"No, I...I was thinking, we should talk."

I sigh. "Yeah, we probably should. I was just thinking, too."

"You were?"

"I need this to work out, Scarlett. You know that. But I think seeing my brothers tonight brings that home."

"You're already rich," she says softly, "are they worth that much?"

I take a long swallow of my drink. "I think I made the right decision in choosing you." With a laugh, I shake my head. "And yeah, it was quick, but...you know, it's not about money. It's about family. History. It's about legacy to me. They were important to the family right at the beginnings of everything. That's important to me. And..."

I trail off. I've said more than I mean to. I've drunk more than I planned, and that buzz is still in my blood. But her face. She's frozen, looking...I don't know, like she just took all the cookies and ate them to hide them.

"Scarlett?"

"The thing is," she says, "I need to tell you something."

Fuck. I wait.

"I really like you and—"

I lean into her and kiss her softly. "Don't. Don't spoil anything by adding to that. Okay? You know where I stand. I like you, too. But that's all it is. Like, attraction. Hormones."

"Hudson..." She takes a breath. "I just wanted to say—"

"We should go dancing."

She's about to continue, but her mouth snaps shut. Then she downs her drink and says, "Do what now?"

"Dance?" Oh, yeah, I'm definitely feeling a little fine from the booze. And from her presence. "What were you going to say?"

"It can wait," she says. "I want to see you dance. Is there an old fashioned, old timey place here?"

I know exactly what she's hinting at and she's pushing it, but I just nod, say yes and lead her out of the bar.

Scarlett can't dance.

She's got it in her, but no one taught her.

I pull her in and guide her through the dance, my mouth at her ear, the music thrumming its rich, evocative beat through our bones in the dark, packed club. "Let go, Scarlett," I murmur, feeling her shiver in my arms as I move my hips against her, taking her with me in a sweet slide of a step that's more like fucking than dancing. "Just let the beat take you. Let me lead you."

Her fingers at my nape dig in and I like the bite. "When you said dancing, I thought you meant waltz."

"That has an eroticism all its own, too, if you know what you're doing."

"We're at a salsa club. Who are you and what have you done with Hudson?"

I laugh and her face burrows into my chest a moment.

"My mother made us all learn to be rounded. My father stated it was a waste of time but she was adamant, and she made us do it all. Hell, I think there was a stint in the boy scouts. But this…I don't do it often."

Make that almost never these days, but back in my college life, fuck yes.

"It's not dancing."

It wasn't. This was definitely foreplay. It could be as good as sex and she was hot and soft and now looking at me with hungry eyes.

I want to say I'm drunk and that's why I'm going to do what I'm planning. I want to find a place to park all the excuses.

I'm a little toasty, but in perfect control. I'm choosing not to be. Because she's there and she's what I want.

I slide my hand that's on her hip down to her ass and bring her in flush against me.

She gasps a little, her fingers digging deeper and she moves against me.

"It's seduction, Scarlett. Or a precursor."

And I kiss her. It's a slow dance of a kiss, highly erotic, and my cock gets harder as she kisses me back with all that she is.

Her mouth is soft, hot, and sweet, that wicked kind with bite, and her tongue definitely knows how to dance. It does so, slow and dirty, against mine. It's the kind of kiss that is pure filth, filled with promises that can be delivered. The sweaty, orgasmic kind.

I pull back, a deliberate tease that has her seeking out my mouth and I kiss her again, the corner of her mouth and then down, along that slender column of throat, to her beating artery, and I suck it. She grinds in against me, the pulse in my mouth going wild and hard and then I let go, and bite, and lick and make my way back to her mouth where I take it hard, open, in an explicit dance of sex.

If I don't stop, I'm going to come right here.

And right or wrong, I'm going to do it. I'm going to cross the line into the next level.

With her.

I lift my head. "Come home with me."

Chapter Sixteen

SCARLETT

This man can kiss. He can kiss a woman right out of her clothes and into his bed. Even if she was a forever kinda girl who knows he's only a sex kind of guy.

Lucky for me, I'm not a forever kinda girl. At least, I'm not a forever *yet* kinda girl.

My mind is spinning and the thoughts are jumbled, coming thick and fast and I'm in a haze caused by him and that thing he called dancing, but was pretty much vertical sex with all your clothes on.

I should know this complicated doing makes things, well, more complicated but I'm not turning down what promises to be the world's best candy.

The music moves through my bones, vibrates in my blood, just like he does, and his not question is still in the air.

There's so much I need to do. Talk to him. I slide my hands up his T-shirt, the hard, sculpted muscles under my palms hot and damp and in the low lighting I know what I have to do.

Tell him why I asked him to come out. Tell him the truth.

After all, that was my plan, the reason I'm here, and to back it all up with the words it doesn't change a thing. I'm still there for him.

It's the right thing to do.

I rise on my toes, our mouths so close, and I take a breath.

Then I kiss him, push my lips to his and they give way and our tongues tangle and he sweeps me into him, harder than before, and that erection is big and solid and straining against me. And I want it. I want him.

He's down deep inside me, the kiss is everywhere, making all my nerves sing and dance and swoon.

We're on top of each other and it isn't enough. I break the kiss and I whisper, "Yes."

His hand is light on my thigh as we drive back to Manhattan. Of course, it's a car service. He's that kind of guy, even though we've been in a cab before. And I'll bet whatever small change I have that this is his own private service.

What I should be doing, I tell myself as the tension grows thick, the anticipation charged and sex laden, is do what I haven't done.

Tell him.

But those plans went out the window when he told me how much this all meant to him. They grew wings and flew like giant birds when I couldn't or didn't find a place to tell him and continue not to. And now...now I'm going to his place and we're going to...

I swallow, hard.

Have sex.

He links his fingers with mine and it's all so new and familiar and everything is spinning fast and low.

It takes a small forever and it takes no time at all to make it from Brooklyn to his east side home. No time at all to wait for him to open the door and step into the low darkness of a place that smells like him and beeswax and lemon and spice.

It's going to be fine, I tell myself. I can't let him down and I'm not going to. My guilt can just stay like that. Or I can drop clues like I'm Gretel and—

"Scarlett."

His voice stops all logic flowing to my brain. It's low and black velvet and full of the sort of promises that are adults only.

I look at him.

And he smiles.

It's slow and hot and predatory and I'm melting.

Hudson's arm slides about me and he kisses me.

This kiss is hard, and it steals breath and bones and replaces it all with fire and liquid need. I'm slammed up against the door and it's a carnal feast and I'm absolutely ravenous.

He makes his way down my throat as his free hand slides up my thigh. "Are you sure?"

I suck in a gasping breath, my fingers tangled in his hair. "Yes!"

And through the trousers I'm wearing he slides against the juncture there, up against my pussy and I'm hot everywhere and throbbing, and I push into those questing fingers, just to back myself up.

"This could complicate things."

Why is he talking? I'm not here to talk. "Or make them more believable."

"You have a point." And his teeth sink lightly into the sensitive skin at the top of my breast, through my shirt and I'm sure my eyes roll back in my head at the exquisite bolt of desire it sends ricocheting through my flesh. Right to my clit.

"Of course I have a point," I say, grabbing his head and pulling it up and kissing him with everything I am. His mouth opens and is just as nakedly sexual, the need in him just as raw and wild as the need that courses through me.

I push him back and he lets me. I know he does. It's the only reason I can do that. I'm beyond trying to work out how this Hudson fits with the Hudson who wears a suit and lines up all his ducks with the precision of a general, only that it does. Too well.

I push him and I push him again until I have him back against the wall to the right. I'm not paying attention to anything but him, and things clatter to the ground. His eyes glitter with hunger as he watches and waits and I move in.

"You talk too much, Hudson," I say, sliding my hands down over his chest, pushing one under the T-shirt, and fuck if his skin isn't like hot silk over steel. I wonder if it's like that everywhere, and I intend to find out, especially that package that strains against his jeans.

"I do?"

"Yes." I wonder how his cock looks, how it tastes, and I know I want it in my mouth, in my pussy. I want to just be consumed by him. Invaded.

"That's rich."

"Excuse me?" I trail my other hand lower, over the buttons of his jeans and oh, yes, there he is. Hard. Hot. Big. He's so big and that's all for me.

He grabs my hand and holds it there. "You accusing me of talking too much. I can barely get you to shut up." There's no rancor in his tone, only heat and hunger. "You better know what you want, Scarlett."

"You." The word is immediate. True. "All of you. Now."

He kisses me again, keeping my hand against his hard cock, and this time the kiss is deceptively soft. But the vibration of dark hunger that's there turns my temperature all the way up. "We should get started."

We're walking, or he's guiding me to something. A soft ding tells me it's an elevator and then we're in it. If I wasn't so consumed by lust and need and desire I'd be floored by the fact he has an elevator in his home. But right now, I'm only floored by him.

Hudson is looking at me, and somehow, just by us standing there, not even kissing now, looking at each other, my hand held against his cock by his, it's the most erotic and charged moment of my life.

When the elevator dings again, he lifts my hand away and brings it to his mouth and he deliberately sucks my thumb, biting down on the pad, sending a jolt of pure erotic energy through me, and then he leads me out, smart lighting blooming as we go.

My hand is in his now, and he takes me down the wide hall with art on the wall that I don't even bother to look at. There are doors leading off each side but at the end of the short hall we come to a wide-open door.

This time, he reaches out and does something just inside the door and the lighting comes on at his touch.

Hudson turns to me. "Last chance."

"For what?"

"To run."

"I'm not going to run. Do I look like a runner? No. Besides, you're drunk and I'm here to take advantage of it."

"I'm not drunk, Scarlett." He moves in close, dropping my hand as he cradles my face with both of his hands. "I had a few, but I'm in complete control."

"Why are we talking?"

He smiles slow and kisses me. Soft, once, and I'm on him, hands under his shirt and he's on me, tugging at the buttons of my shirt, down to the side zip of the trousers I'm wearing and the kisses grow hot and hard as each article of clothing comes off.

And then he's against me. Flesh against flesh and he is a living specimen of male fantasy. His hands are on my hips as he thrusts against me, letting me know his need and then he pushes me back and I go, landing on something soft and big—the bed. I'm paying absolutely zero attention to the room we're in. Everything I do is focused on him and the need and urgency growing.

The lighting is a low and soft glowing amber, and the room is big like the bed and he lands on me, pushes my thighs apart with one hand, his mouth hot once more on mine. This time the kisses are drugging and long and deep, the type to sink into, and reach for more.

And his fingers on my thigh are a whispering tease as they slip higher until he's stroking the lips of my pussy, light and feathery. I'm wet, I'm aching. It's that deep, throbbing ache that needs to be assuaged by him inside me.

Back and forth he goes, building a rhythm, one of his thighs pinning one of mine so I'm spread open to him and half trapped. His cock is there, and hot and erect, and I need to touch it.

I reach down and wrap my fingers around the thick girth and tease the head with my thumb and he growls low in the back of his throat.

His fingers tease higher, just to my clit, not quite touching, and I try to move to them, to have him on my sensitive bud, but he just laughs, and I give him a squeeze.

"Hungry girl." I do it again, teasing him back, this time pumping him slow and using the precum to slide back and forth over the head of his cock.

"You keep that up," he mutters in my ear, one of his fingers pushing into my wetness, between the folds and into my pussy and I convulse, little butterfly wings of an orgasm around that sweet invasion, "and this is going to be all you're getting for a while."

"Are you saying you'll be coming in your pant—oh!—pants."

The fucker does it again, pushing in with another finger, staying shy of my clit, and he thrusts in and out, giving me a taste of real satisfaction but holding it from me like some sadistic creature.

"I'm not wearing pants." He punctuates each word with small bites on my throat, accompanied by a thrust of his fingers into me.

"Just—oh, God..." I'm writhing as he now begins a measured assault around my clit, not quite going for that nirvana I need. "Just fuck me, Hudson."

"Your pussy is so tight and wet. I bet it tastes sweet. Do you?"

"I'm not that flexible."

He laughs and pulls his fingers from me, and then my hand from his cock and he moves down me, kissing and licking a trail over my burning skin, until he reaches my pussy.

Hudson licks me. All the way from top to bottom and back again, dipping inside me, sucking my clit into his mouth and teasing it gently with his tongue, and I scream. I actually scream.

My hands are in his hair, tight and I half orgasm, but he pulls away again.

Diabolical bastard. He pulls the fuck away and comes back up me, this time his body on mine, heavy between me, my thighs either side of him and he kisses me and I can taste myself on him.

"Sweet," he says.

I'm too busy drawing up my knees and pushing up with my hips to try to get him to fuck me, to put that thick cock where I need it. I try to reach down, but he stops me, pinning a wrist down to the bed next to us. And then he uses his other hand and pushes his cock against my entrance, once, twice, and then again. Again and again, he pushes right there, my lips moving to take him and again and again he retreats.

"You'll be sweet in tiny pieces if you don't fuck me."

"Vicious," he says, licking along my throat, "aren't you? If only the ladies in the Hamptons could see you now."

"They'd see you, too." I have no idea what he's talking about. I don't care about anything but this. I've gone and lost my mind.

"I don't fucking care if they do."

And this time, he thrusts into me. He's big. I know that from touching him, but when he's pushing his way into me, stretching me wide, filling me, it's a different story. And I'm in heaven.

All words slip away as he pulls my legs up high, so he can thrust hard and deep into me. Inside, I'm coming apart. Each time he slams into me is a revelation and I'm moaning and clutching and moving my hips up to take more of him. I want it all. Everything.

The fullness, the being joined, and it's more than that. It's like coming to a home I never knew I had or needed. And I bite his shoulder to stop from screaming again. He moves faster and inside I'm a tornado of flaming desire. I'm being consumed. Stretched. Opened. Taken.

And the need builds. The tension, the pleasure, starts to combust and then I'm just gone. A cascading firestorm of absolute pleasure as I come, my body convulsing and clamping down on his, over and over again. I'm flying high, I'm nothing but this. And I give over to those waves of heaven.

Finally, I start to come down and Hudson's still thrusting into me. Harder, now. Faster. No control as he's getting close and he's making me come all over again.

I'm rolling with it. It's too much. I'm out of control and I can't find anything but him to cling to and I feel him come and he shudders in my arms, his body emptying into mine, and he kisses me hard as he does so.

Finally, he slumps down. And I'm too exhausted to do anything but wrap my arms and legs around him, with him still inside me, and close my eyes.

That was worth the world.

We have sex three more times. Once so hard I thought the bed would break, another slow and languid and eye-rollingly sensual. And another so filthy I could come again just thinking about it.

I can't sleep.

Hudson is. He's got one arm thrown over me and I've been watching him for what feels like forever, and I could do it for another forever, too.

But I can't.

As all the pleasure and the need has now been satiated, with it comes the commonsense hangover.

I might have justified things to myself before we did all that naked salsa-ing, but how can I now? I came here to tell him the truth now instead of later, when things got complicated.

And now things were definitely complicated.

It's struck me at some point in the last small forever of watching him sleep, the long lashes that dust against his cheeks, the stubble, the softness to his features that isn't there when he's awake, the little huffling snore he makes, that slides into me and warms me down to the toes, it's struck me that I've let things go way too far.

I'm in way too deep with the lies. They might be white, but there are a lot of them and they're growing, and I worry, now we've done that, he won't see it as something small that got out of hand, but something else entirely.

Something darker.

Something he'll want to take revenge on.

I've let things go on and on and on by essentially lying to him every moment of the day.

Slowly, I slide out from under his embrace, careful not to wake him.

The room around me is in darkness, but there's enough light from the window to show me where I am.

A big bedroom. It's not what I expected. It's definitely got money and quality all over it. But it's simple and masculine and comfortable. It's not trying to be anything but what it is, a bedroom with a king-size bed, a bookcase on one wall, and a sofa under the window. There are a couple of plants too. He never struck me as a plant guy, but maybe it's his interior decorator. Although I don't think one did this room. It feels utterly Hudson in a way I can't exactly explain.

I'm standing, naked, writing a soliloquy in my head to his bedroom.

With a shake of my head, I find my clothes and pull them on, heading out the door. There's a staircase straight ahead, past all the other doors and the elevator, and I head to that.

I need to get out of here, get home, and think about what to do next.

My hand is on the railing, when a floorboard creaks behind me and Hudson speaks.

"Going somewhere?"

Chapter Seventeen

HUDSON

If anyone's sneaking out of this kind of situation, it would be me. I don't tend to—I haven't since I was in college. Since then, I've picked wisely and made sure everything is streamlined.

This isn't.

And Scarlett sneaking out like some fucking thief is not what I expect.

I don't know what to expect when it comes to her.

She's a constant surprise.

Especially sex that good.

I knew it would be good—the tension and electricity between us, the kisses too, told me so. But I didn't know it would be that... I don't want to use the word phenomenal, but it's there in my head, anyway.

It's almost five am, and I need to be up in an hour because I'm not one of those rich guys who ride daddy or mommy's coattails and wander into work whenever they feel like it. So, I'm not sure why I'm up and half-dressed, and I'm even less sure why I'm trying to stop her leaving when I could have just turned over and gone back to sleep.

Her hand grips the rail tight. In the half-light her knuckles turn white.

Scarlett turns slowly, and she stares at my chest a long time, then raises her gaze to mine. The desire is still there burning, and it makes my dick start to wake.

"Going home. This...you and me...it isn't a thing."

"Right. So, you sneak off?"

"It's not sneaking." She hesitates, her gaze dipping again, and then she raises her chin. "I'm being sensible."

Rich girls who work but weren't bred to being sensible? She's one bundle of mysteriousness I'd like to delve into. More than I have. I also don't know if I believe her.

Because she looks at me like she doesn't want to go.

She looks at me like she wants to climb back on my cock and ride me.

Yet there she stands, buttoned up and jumpy.

I lean my shoulder against the matte cream wall and slide my hand into the pocket of my half-buttoned jeans that sit low. "Sensible?"

"I need to get home. Get changed, make it look like I didn't have sex half the night. And not be late. My boss hates people who are late."

"He also hates liars," I say softly, and her eyes darken a moment.

It's a perfectly reasonable excuse she's giving me. There are no promises or words of love, and she knows I don't have or give those. But I don't think that's why she's trying to sneak out. And I don't think it's because she wasn't into the sex, not the way her gaze goes to my crotch, and heat streaks up her throat as she licks her lips.

I think she's lying, but I can't for the life of me fathom the reason. Even the guy that made me inexplicably jealous seems a likely culprit. She hasn't mentioned him and there's nothing about her that's indicated she lusts or pines for someone else.

"This isn't part of the contract, Hudson."

"I'm aware."

"Don't you think this complicates it?"

Yes, no. I don't know. "It makes it all the more authentic. And we wanted it."

I put a soft emphasis on the we.

She takes in a breath that's slightly fluttery. "I know, oh, do I know that. But..."

I wait. Wait some more. Scarlett doesn't finish her sentence. If she wasn't holding herself so stiffly, I suspect she might be fluttering like a trapped bird right now.

"But?"

"But I don't want to take advantage of any of this." She basically swallows air and her shoulders rise as she pushes it out with a storm of words. "You know, the job and the contract? You have such high standards and I'm working hard and I don't want to sleep my way to the top. Crap, that came out wrong. You know what I mean. No, you don't. I don't. I guess I'm trying to say I want to just go and get ready and be on time like everything is normal."

I take all that in, dissect it. She doesn't fit any mold I've ever seen or known, and no woman, whether a social climber or socialite or someone who wants to bag a billionaire—and I've seen and side-stepped all of them—would sleep with me and then try to have everything normal and try to still prove she's responsible and good at her job. She'd use this.

Maybe that's cynical, but that's what I've seen. I don't sleep with my staff—until now. And she's a different story. In all ways.

But to have her stand here and say perfectly reasonable things and me think she's lying about...something, is odd.

Because I don't know what the fuck it is.

I appreciate her playing by my rules and taking after my own standards in that respect.

"What's the real deal here, Scarlett?"

For a moment she looks like a terrified rabbit, but it vanishes and she narrows her eyes. "That is the real deal, the hot tea. Lukewarm in this case. I have a job to do and my boss really hates me being late."

She doesn't move, though.

I find that interesting. Just like I find all the pieces here interesting even if there's something wrong with them.

Maybe she feels uncomfortable or maybe she's worried I'll think she's angling for more. But everything we have pays her unbelievably sweetly, and it's all iron clad in my favor.

Nothing about Scarlett since I've met her makes sense in light of what I expected. And it's not my business if there's something going on, or she's got an inner battle to forge. I don't really care, as long as whatever is going on with her doesn't get in the way of what it is I want.

"Do you want to leave?"

She blinks. "I...what do you mean?"

"I think that's a pretty straightforward question," I say with a small smile. "You can go if you want to leave. But do you want to go?"

"I told you about my boss..."

"I have it on good authority he won't mind if you're late today. So take that out. Do you want to go or do you want to get back in bed with me?"

For a moment, I think she's going to turn and leave, but she doesn't. Scarlett walks towards me. "If this is it, then I'll take more."

"Good."

And I pull her to me and kiss her, her hand sliding down into my pants to wrap about my cock. I take her hand away, and it almost kills me to do it, but I have a few other plans if this is the last time, which it needs to be.

In my bedroom, I seduce her out of her clothes and then I go down on her, and let her do the same to me, stopping short each time of coming. I want to be in her when we both come. I want to prolong that sweet agony.

I tumble her to the bed and slide her up over me, positioning my cock at her opening and then I push into that hot, wet tightness, or she pushes down, and we start fucking, slow and sensuous, with a bite to it that tells me everything's going to go haywire again.

It's a good thing I'm the boss because I suspect we're both going to be late today.

Exceptionally late.

For exceptionally good reasons.

"Take the morning off," I say to Scarlett as I finish getting ready.

She's dressed and a part of me is surprised after her quick shower that she didn't bolt when I was in guest one, taking my own.

Instead, she's perched on the couch in the bedroom, looking all levels of uncomfortable at the situation, staring at her phone, waiting, it seems, for me.

I'm not exactly sure why I pointed her to my shower as there is a guest one just next door, but I did. And it's not intimate getting dressed, as the walk-in closet is also a dressing room and that's what I've done, gone in there after my shower and dressed.

It's not intimate, but there's something about it, having her there that makes this almost a familial closeness, like we're a unit.

Something, I tell myself, to add to the authenticity of it all, because there will be questions.

She looks up at me as I walk out, fully dressed in my suit, and there's an array of interesting expressions flitting over her face that range from desire to embarrassment to doubtfulness, the last complete with a frown.

Her hair is pulled back, which I don't miss the meaning of. Not that she needs to do that with me. Last night was then and this is real life.

She gets to her feet. "I can't, you have—"

"Take the morning off." I put in the last cufflink. "You can work late if you feel the need. But everything's running smoothly and I've got meetings all day."

She nods then, her professional face on.

Turning, I usher her out of the bedroom and into the hall. Anyone else would have snooped about or been disgruntled by the difference in my behavior. Not Scarlett. If anything, she seems a little relieved it's business as usual and I'm...I'm not exactly sure how I feel about that.

I probably should go over everything again, the whole that was then and this is now, but before I can decide to, the elevator whooshes open and Ryder is there with to-go coffees and a bag that smells like a heavenly heart attack in butter and pastry.

"You shouldn't give your door code out to just anyone," he's saying. "*I* came in...oh *Hello*."

He stops, staring at Scarlett who goes red.

Ryder thrusts the coffee and pastries at me and I grab them before they can spill as he cranes his neck to see past me and down into the bedroom and then he runs a practiced eye over Scarlett, as if he has no idea who she is.

"Well aren't you the dark horse, Hud. Making things official?"

"I need to go," she says, like she's been caught doing something she shouldn't. "Nice seeing you again—"

"Ryder, the sexier, better brother." He grins at me, but it fades quickly into something else. "Look, you might want to stay, too."

I glance at her and she sighs, staying where she is. The pit of my stomach tightens and all the goodness from sex seeps away, taking with it any residual languidness that might be still lingering in my bones.

"Ryder," I say, handing him the damn pastries and coffee, my voice low and dangerous. "What the fuck are you on about?"

"I wasn't flirting with your girl, just messing with you."

"She's not my girl," I say at the same time she says, "I'm not anyone's girl."

For some reason, that irritates me but I ignore it. Lack of sleep is my issue here, and my brother seemingly dropping in on a workday. For all I know, Ryder drops by every day and I'm gone, but I don't think so.

And I don't want her to be my girl and I don't want her thinking she is for some insane reason. Why he'd say that is beyond me, too.

I shift my brain back to the issue at hand.

My brother.

Here on a mission.

"I'm talking, Ryder, about the other shit. Why you said Scarlett needed to stay."

"I said might." He offers a coffee to Scarlett, who takes it, looking completely thrown and there's that something in her face I don't quite get, that makes me a little off-center.

Then again, it could be Ryder. But he's not looking happy, either.

"Okay," he says, "fine. I put word out, found someone to pay off to get me any information from Jenson's office about this."

He doesn't even have the grace to look embarrassed. He never has when it's come to him wanting things. What he can't get through charm and underhanded maneuvers, he'll do the old-fashioned way: with cold, hard cash.

"What did you find?" I know he went looking for information on the jewels. That's him all over. The mystery is alive again, realer than it ever was, and of course he'd try and find out all he could.

"Nothing more about the Sinclair jewels."

"Not surprising, seeing as I saw you last night. And you already told me what you knew."

Scarlett's standing there, holding the coffee she clearly doesn't want, looking how I feel. I catch her gaze and there's a world of questions there I can't even begin to answer. But I've got a feeling I'm not going to like whatever it is my brother's going to say next.

"Yeah, but..."

"But?" I wait.

Ryder sighs. "But this isn't as easy as you thought."

"What does that mean?" Scarlett's voice is tight, with panic just beneath the surface. "I need to give a kidney?"

"Worse," he mutters.

"We need to get married for real?"

I raise an eyebrow at the horror in her voice. "That's not happening. But it wouldn't be the worst thing."

"Really?" Ryder's looking at me with real interest.

They are both beginning to annoy me. For very different reasons. Scarlett's intimation it would be a fate worse than death is insulting and Ryder's expression... But I push that away, and I mutter, "Fake engagement, fake marriage, whatever. It's a piece of paper and fixable. What's the issue here?"

"Right, right." He pulls a croissant out of the bag and takes a bite, chews, and swallows. And I'm ready to throttle him. "There's going to be a test, Hudson."

"I figured," I say.

"For both of you."

"Again, I kind of figured it wouldn't be as simple as here's my fiancé. Give me what's mine."

Ryder breathes out slowly and he looks me in the eye. "There's more to it, Hud. Seems if you don't pass, it's not only that you don't get what you want, it seems that Sinclair, the family flagship, our birthright, it seems that might well be lost, too."

His mouth thins. "To all of us."

Chapter Eighteen

SCARLETT

The word horror seems way too pallid a word to describe how I feel.

I mean, Hudson has said this is important, but his brother's words change things. And I don't want to be there for that.

If this falls apart because of little white lies, he loses part of himself.

That sounds melodramatic, but it's true.

And it would be my fault.

My screw up.

My little white lies.

I try to stall to talk to him, but he's looking at his watch and shaking his head. And I don't catch what they say to each other through the roaring in my head. I want to faint or hyperventilate or scream.

But I don't. I am a monolith of strength. Well, I keep it together as he hustles us all into the elevator and out onto the street.

Hudson turns to me, not looking overly concerned, but that's him. He's got that kind of poker face. The morning sun catches his dark hair and makes it shine. I swallow, remembering how it was damp with sweat last night when I gripped tightly when he was— "Do you want a car?"

"No!" I blurt the word, trying to rid myself of memories that have no right appearing right now. They're not a help.

And his brother is watching us both a little too closely for my liking.

"You don't want a car? To get home?"

"No. I do not. Not a car." I'm panicking and I shouldn't be. Shit.

Hudson cracks a small smile and takes the coffee from me. "I'm not getting you a jet or a helicopter. Seems a little excessive."

I scowl and cross my arms. "I don't feel comfortable getting in a car."

What I need is to take a shovel with me to make digging these holes easier.

"They've had them for years now. Safe enough," Ryder says with too much cheer. "Surely you've been in one."

"Shut up, Ryder," Hudson says. "Don't you have work to do?"

"I'll give her a lift—"

"I'm fine." I take a big step back. "I—it's a lovely morning, so I'll walk." To the train. And I throw a small thanks to whatever deity is watching that it isn't raining. I look at Hudson as a sleek car pulls up as he takes a sip of the coffee. "Can we talk? Later?"

"Scarlett."

The warning note throws me, and I realize how my words sound. Or, rather, how he interpreted them. Asshole.

Hudson's so handsome, so sure I meant another romp in bed. Which I didn't. I wouldn't turn it down, but... As I look at him, if it was to come up, I know I should. He is handsome. The best looking man I've ever seen, which is saying something because his brother is also gorgeous. But Hudson is different.

"Talk talk," I say.

"If I have time. You know my schedule."

I sort of want to scream. There he is, this news sitting there, hand delivered by his brother, and he's so closed and untouchable, like he often is, and it hurts and I don't know why.

"It's just I figured if there's more riding on this, then we should. Talk. If you have time."

"Sure," he says, but he's not paying attention to me, not really.

The sun is already warm and there are people walking their dogs and this is about as bucolic as New York gets, so I make my goodbyes and take off.

At least getting to Brooklyn in the am is much easier than the other way. But the car would have been a boon. One I couldn't risk. If I accepted, then he'd know I'd be going to Brooklyn and not a short ride to the other side of the park.

Once home, I jump in the shower again and dress like I'm some matron aunt going into corporate battle. And I grab a slice of bread and race out again and make it to the office before ten am.

I throw myself into my work. There are calls and emails and suits to send out and pick up and all the little bits and pieces. Through it all, I try to concentrate.

The day passes both slow and fast. I've been feeling sick to my stomach the entire time. It lurches and turns when all that happened slams into me. And when I'm not thinking about the whole meaning of his brother's words, it churns away, anyway.

I haven't been able to check my phone, but I know there are a number of messages as before I turned it off there were little icons showing me emails and missed calls and texts. Lunch is something I forget about as I work through that hour, and the only good thing which might not be a good thing is I don't see Hudson. He's busy until early evening.

Being a billionaire isn't yachts and sun and swimwear models, it's hard work, at least for my billionaire. I mean my pretend billionaire. He's a billionaire, but he's not mine, that's what I mean.

And...all this work has saved me thinking too much about that insanely phenomenal sex that when flashes come to me, I melt and feel the need to fan myself.

I end up staying until almost seven, which isn't unheard of when people work for Hudson Sinclair—it seems to be part of the job, actually, but not for me when he's not here. I think it's guilt.

The evening is a little cooler than the day, and I switch on my phone as I head out. By the time I'm disembarking the elevator in the grand foyer of the building, I've been bombarded by messages from my brother and it seems he's beside himself about something. I shoot him a text and then I jump in a cab and head to the Lower East Side to meet him.

I get off the F train at Delancey and Essex and make my way to the little bar. It used to be a dive, but now it's tapas and wine.

Danny is looking at his phone at a little table in the back, a brooding, dark expression on his handsome face as he hunches down, ignoring his wine.

I swipe it and take a deep swallow, like it contains the answers to everything or at the very least, some courage.

Danny tosses his phone on the powder black steel table and glares. "You're still alive."

"What happened?"

I pull my feet up under my chair right after I sit down, one hand still wrapped about his wine glass.

"I'm done."

"What? Danny, what happened?"

My brother doesn't answer for a long time. Then finally he says, "Adam."

I've been so caught up in my own issues, even if they came about to try and help him, that I haven't checked up on him. And guilt for that suddenly swamps me. He lost almost everything when his partner double crossed him and made it look like it was all Danny. I'd do anything to help. Except, it seems, be there.

"Adam? I thought things were now separated. Oh, Danny, you didn't leave something hanging, did you?"

He frowns, snatching back his wine. "I'm not a complete idiot. Even if it seems like it. And I'm not eighteen and careless anymore."

I breathe out and order a drink as the waitress comes by. Just a house red. Danny holds up his glass to her and she's off. I turn back to my brother.

"What happened?"

He stares at the table a moment, then lays his palms flat against it and looks at me. "We should be talking about you and Hudson Sinclair."

"No, we shouldn't," I say. "It's just a fill-in job, that's all."

He's stalling and I don't know why. Whatever it is, it's bad. When his so-called partner went out on his own, he burned Danny's reputation down, badmouthing him and laying everything he'd done on Danny's doorstep. And through it all, Danny's tried to pick up the pieces and continue on, to rebuild.

But New York is tough when you're borderline blackballed, and someone with power and reputation isn't there in your corner.

"What happened?"

"Me first," he says. "Then you."

I slide one hand to my lap and cross my fingers. "Okay."

He sighs heavily. "I'm gonna lose my office."

"Shit, Danny. I'm sorry. Can you work from home?"

"And how's that going to look for me?"

He's right. The waitress returns with our drinks and when she goes, Danny pins me with a look. "Your turn."

"What?"

"This Sinclair job?"

I hesitate. In the low light and laid-back atmosphere of the bar, I feel like I'm under bright bodega lighting. But I know I owe him something. Just he's proud and if I tell him the truth, he'll tell me to go away, but with the threat of losing his office I can't do that. If he hasn't lost it already. He said going to, not has. It gives me a dubious smidge of hope.

"It's just temporary—"

"You were with Hudson Sinclair."

I swallow and push the toes of my shoes down against the ground beneath my seat, as if that will give me courage. Or strength. Or something. "It's a temporary job with him. I got it through a friend. To help her out."

"Not that flighty one you sometimes have drinks with—"

"Danny, we need to leave it."

"And what about what you want to do?"

I shrug. "It's not like there are people knocking on my door. And—"

"Scarlett." Danny grabs my arm, his expression intense. "I know you're up to something. You don't belong in his world. Not in a corporate setting. You've always said so."

"Things change—"

"Not that much," he says. "I'm not an idiot. He's real estate. Oh, Christ, this isn't about me, is it?"

"No!" I'm crossing my fingers hard.

"I'm saying it again. I know you're up to something. If you're trying to trick or manipulate a Sinclair into whatever the hell is going on in your brain, stop. They are ruthless. Hudson Sinclair comes across as a nice guy, but he's ruthless, too, when he wants to be. He turned us down once when we went to him to try and get in under the Sinclair name, did you know that?"

"Look, Danny, I'm not…I'm not trying to trick him." This is true. I'm not. It just sort of happened. I down my drink, almost choking on the wine as I lay some money down on the table, pulling it from my bag I flung on the table. "I have to go. I'm okay—"

"Wait." He's still holding my arm. "There's something you don't know. When…when Adam did all that shit to those people, and we got turned down, he tried to steal business from Hudson Sinclair."

I hiss out a breath. My stomach turns sour. "What? Why didn't you tell me?"

"Because I don't know. I was ashamed?"

"I don't think he knows who you are."

But Danny's mouth thinned. "These Sinclair brothers have a way of getting back at people and maybe he found out. Or maybe he thinks it's still Adam, but you know who's behind turfing people out of the building?"

He doesn't need to say it. He doesn't.

But he does.

"Hudson Sinclair."

I'm in a state when I leave the bar.

Hudson buys and sells and owns so many places that the little downtown building where Danny rents from would be so low on his list of things that it's probably just something he's moving about. Property-wise.

Still…

I might be able to do something, I just don't know what yet.

And to make matters worse, as I leave, there's a text from the man himself.

I'll meet you at your place in two hours.

This isn't anything other than an order. And I rush home to change and rush out again, barely saying hi to Amber as I fly in and out.

The panic is huge now. Overwhelming.

If this was someone else, the late hour would send thrills through me. This is Hudson. He's getting out of a business dinner.

And there's one thing to talk about: what his brother told us.

Okay, I need to tackle one issue at a time. That's all.

And the first one is getting to Sarah's before him.

For once, all the subway gods are smiling on me and I get there with half an hour to spare.

I bound up the steps and run into someone.

He's tall. Solid. Smells good. He makes me melt normally.

Hudson.

Shit.

I find a smile and aim it up at him, but he fails to smile back. His eyes are almost black.

"You're early," I say. "I just had to go grab something and—"

"Cut the fucking bullshit, Scarlett," he says quietly, coolly. "I know you don't live here. Explain."

Chapter Nineteen

HUDSON

She looks at me, wide eyed. And then smiles and tries to bluster her way out of it with healthy heapings of charm.

"What? Of course I do. Did you hit your head?" She bites her lip and takes hold of my arms and looks up at me. "What do you mean?"

"I mean, Scarlett, I had a long chat with the doorman and you don't live here."

"He's new."

I narrow my eyes, refusing to let the charm get to me as people give us strange looks as they go past into and out of the building and I really don't give a flying fuck. This day got way too long the moment my brother dropped his little bombshell.

"To you, twenty-five years working at this building is classed as new?"

She smiles, but there's a desperation there I don't like. "In some cultures."

"I don't have time for this, Scarlett. Didn't I tell you I don't want lies?" I shake my head and pull free of her, regret bitter in my mouth and confusion in my veins. Why lie about something like this, that's what I want to know, but it's something she needs to share with me.

"I know. You did. But, after this morning..." She twists her hands in front of her and this isn't the place for this.

"I'll see you tomorrow, Scarlett. Usual time." I walk away from the entrance and cross the pavement to where my car waits and get in.

Once there, I lean back on the leather seat and close my eyes. My driver won't go anywhere until I tell him to. And I need to think.

I want to get out and go back to Scarlett and put my hands on her. But if I do that, I know exactly where that will lead because she's a fever in my blood. Last night and the very early hours of this morning weren't enough.

But I want to grab hold and demand the truth.

That's not going to work. I know that. If she wants to explain all this without trying to wiggle out of it, she needs to come to me.

It's not that important in the grand scale of things, I suppose, but it does make me wonder... If she's lied about this, what else has she lied about?

The door opens and the noise and warm air of New York invades the car, along with Scarlett.

I know it's her. I can feel her there, a buzz in my blood, a heat on my skin. Her soft breathing is a call to me, too. And I gather my self-control, open my eyes, and look at her.

"I'm not lying, not really," she says. "My family—"

"Scarlett." She's pretty, even in a panic, the color high on her cheeks, her hair still back but little wisps are like honeyed gold, dark and beautiful around her face. But I make myself ignore the physical attributes and push on. "You were there this morning. You know what's riding on this."

"I know." Her hand is soft as she touches my arm and I like the feel of her, the connection. I shouldn't, but I do.

I look at her hand and then at her and damn if I can't smell those flowers again. But the look has the desired effect and she snatches her hand away.

"We're running out of time," I say, "especially now. We need to be on the same page and move things along."

Scarlett nods and bites her lip. Then she leans forward. "We have, don't you think?"

"Sex?" I laugh. "That's got nothing to do with it."

"I didn't mean the sex." The irritation is strong in her voice and it makes me want to smile, but I don't, because down deep I'm pissed off with her for such a stupid lie.

"Then what did you mean?"

"The moving things along, getting to know each other, hanging out. You know..."

"No, I don't. This is a transaction. I blurred lines I shouldn't have to scratch an itch I should have ignored, no matter how good that was, but Scarlett, if we're moving things along and you're lying to me about something so simple, what else are you lying about?"

She goes pale. "People don't always tell the truth about where they live. Especially when..." She swallows and looks at her hands. "Especially when they're doing this. For money. Because they can't afford to live here."

I look at her and touch her now. I shouldn't, I know, but that pull goes both ways and I've got myself under control enough to use it. I brush my knuckles slow and light along her cheek and then with my other hand draw her in closer, so our mouths almost touch. I can feel her like a beat in my blood, almost taste her again.

It's a dangerous little game I've decided to play, but she's not good at controlling her emotions, so I'm going to use that.

Her breath comes in little, short erratic bursts and her pupils dilate, and it takes real effort not to sample her mouth, just to make sure it's as soft and sweet and ripe as it was this morning.

"Even with money problems," I murmur, "your family has places all over Manhattan."

"Hudson, please..."

"Please what? Kiss you? Let it go?"

That mouth is a siren's song.

And her tongue touches the bottom lip, wetting it and the sight and what it sets off in my imagination makes me hard.

"Don't humiliate me."

"I'm not." I slide my thumb over her bottom lip, along that tiny patch of wetness, wanting to dip inside. "I already know your situation, I'm just asking a question to understand. You put this place down as your address."

"I...it's a family place, but I don't live there. I wanted you to think so."

"I see."

I did. Sort of. Her weirdness about me getting her a car to take her home now made sense. But why the hell would she hide where she lived from me unless that guy was part of it, the one she called Danny, the one who looked familiar for some reason...

"Hudson, look, I...I'm sorry. I am."

I run my finger over her lips. And she sighs. The sound is soft and slides right through me as she leans further into my touch.

"We're meant to be falling in love," I say. The words are a little too easy, but I clarify. "On paper, and to the right people watching. So, it's decision time for me."

She frowns, pulling back a little, her hand now on my thigh, fingers suddenly tight. "What do you mean?"

"I need to decide whether to end this now or continue." It's hard to concentrate with her touching me, even if it's not a sexual thing, because I'm still touching her and she does things to me, reaches in, and the line between me using this and me being tangled gets finer by the second.

"Hudson..." She takes a breath. "I—"

"This is very important to me and you know that." The temperature in the air should be cooling fast with my words, but her proximity makes it rise. "And now it's become even more important than I thought. If I go forward and you screw it up, I lose more than I ever thought. And if I back out now..."

"You lose."

"Maybe. That would be on my terms."

"No, Hudson," she says, the fire in her voice stirring my blood. "You don't give up. You need me to do this."

I did. Like it or not, if I walked now, with half the time gone, finding a replacement would be beyond suspicious and— Shit. I've got myself in deep.

"We're not on the same page, Scarlett. And we have to be if we're going to move it along. Yet here you are, lying about something simple."

"Where I live doesn't matter. This isn't for the government or the police."

I need time that I don't have to think this through. I need her to play my game. I need...I need Scarlett. "It matters to me. If I can't trust you over that, or you can't trust me enough to tell me where you actually live, then it won't work. I demand total honesty, I told you that."

She scoots closer to me on the big, wide leather car seat. We're in our own private cocoon here, one of the benefits of my own bespoke town car. Scarlett searches my face. "No one is totally honest, that's not how things work."

It is in my world. Relationships are messy. Fake ones, it seems, included.

"It does here," I say quietly. "It's who I am, Scarlett. To do this properly, I need that from you, because they'll sniff out something wrong in this fucking interview."

"Hudson..."

"Scarlett, just tell me. What's it going to be?"

Chapter Twenty

SCARLETT

It's the perfect opportunity to tell him. Everything. To just come clean and hope for the best.

Okay, not hope, because that's the kind of wishy-washy thing he doesn't like. Hudson likes plans and smart moves, and coming clean would normally be just that. And with everything that's happened between us, by the way he's touching me, looking at me like he wants another taste, I could work that.

Use my actual brain, solve the problem by coming up with a smart answer for him.

But I can't.

All actions like that come with a risk, and risk is one thing I can't do. Not now. Not after what Danny told me.

If Hudson turned me down, broke the contract, then I'd have zero money. I've read the fine print. Oh, I'd get the pay for the work at the office, but the rest? The real payout, the one I want for Danny? The one I now need for him? No. Not a cent.

And, just as bad as that is this: we're in this now. Deep enough that the time count to what he wants doesn't leave him room. He can walk away, yes, but he won't have time to find someone else to do this now. I'm trapped.

And I need not to be.

I need to think. I slide my hand up from his thigh, over his hard chest that lies beneath the elegant suit, and twist my fingers into the tie and draw myself up close. His fingers are still cradling my face, but no longer doing that sublime and distracting dance against my lips.

"Are you trying to seduce me, Scarlett?"

His voice is low, dark velvet, quietly dangerous, and it's a calling to my blood. I know this can get away from me, fast. "No."

If I was a different kind of woman, a femme fatale, one of the sleek, effortlessly elegant women he no doubt slept with, I'd ask if he wanted me to.

But I don't have the chutzpah for that. Instead, I close the gap and kiss him slow.

And he lets me.

A quiet exploration of a kiss, where I taste his lips, lick a path of my own, dip inside, pressing into him. He lets me. But he doesn't kiss me back. My heart thumps hard in my chest, my pulse lurching. I'm not glamorous or powerful. I'm just me. But I know he wants me. The dark and hungry looks he's given...his kisses and touches and the sex. Oh my God, the sex.

I know he wants me for some reason.

I don't know why.

He could have his pick of any woman. And maybe it's because I'm different or maybe it's because I'm there and time is short and it's smarter for him to use my attraction to make this seem real. I don't know. But I'm ashamed to say, even if it's the latter, then I'll take it.

What that makes me I'm not sure, but I'm getting off track. I'm trying to find a way to give him the right words and to save my brother and get my money.

But as I've said, it's more than that. It's also for him. If this falls to pieces now, no one gets what they want, including Hudson and...I promised I'd help.

I pull back but his hand comes up from my cheek to my hair and he holds me there, right in kissing distance and I can see the stubble that's starting to form, feel the warmth of his breath on my lips as he looks at me.

"Here's the thing. I like you, Scarlett. I'm not in the habit of fucking women I don't like on some level. But you can't use that. Others have tried and failed. Others with way more...experience than you."

I narrow my eyes. "By experience, I'm assuming you mean they're more talented."

"Did I say that?"

"You didn't have to."

He half smiles, drawing me back in, "Not what I meant at all. I meant...actually, it doesn't matter, because games and manipulation and seduction, they aren't going to work on me. I told you. Love doesn't exist. And passion and need and attraction are physical things to be either ignored or indulged in. I can go either way." His gaze drops now, to my lips. "No matter how difficult ignoring that can sometimes be."

His words make my stomach somersault and I almost blurt out everything, but I grab hold of myself and pull back from that dangerous edge. "We can make this work."

"You lied."

"So I don't live here, as I said—"

"I need to trust you in everything going forward, Scarlett. I told you that. Going in circles is a waste of my time."

I know what the answer is, but it's just as dangerous as that precipice, that edge.

"You're right. I don't want to waste my time, either. Hudson, we need to up the ante."

"That's what I said."

I slide up and onto his lap and that hard on is there as I straddle him, half surprised he's letting me do it, and half drunk on the whole bold move.

"What are you doing?"

I take his face in both hands, that strong, lean, gorgeous face. "What do you think? I'm upping the ante."

"Or taking it down."

I push against him and he half groans, his hand in my hair tightening as his other one comes up to my waist to hold me there, pressed in against him.

"Or maybe you're just playing a dangerous game."

"We've already had sex, Hudson, so we should use that."

"And fuck now? Your ante is all over the place."

"And your cock is hard."

"Physical reaction, like I said. I'm attracted to you." He moves his hand down to my throat and half circles it, his thumb teasing against my carotid artery. "What are you up to?"

"I'm saying we use this. Use it, this attraction, when we're out, when we're in the meeting, we can make this happen and…" I take a breath. "You'll be okay."

I'm babbling and I know it, and this time, when I kiss him to buy myself time, he kisses me back and all thought goes south.

It's a powerhouse of a kiss, and the moment our tongues touch, the gentleness in how I began is gone, and it's electrifying hunger. It burned in my veins and the kiss is pure sex, need, desire. All dark and wild, a storm that's just him and me and we both know where it goes.

He takes over, his fingers sliding through my hair, back to my throat, and then down, over my breast, lingering, and he uses his other to bring me into tight, hard contact with his erection. And I throb with need. It's a pressure within, tightly coiled, full of desire that knows what he can do, and I can't help myself. I rub against him, and I know I'm getting wet.

My hands are in his hair and I'm kissing him with everything I am. All of it. Like I can come just from this.

And then he stops kissing me. Hudson lets go of me and pulls my hands from him, taking them down and he holds them by the wrists, behind my back.

His hair is mussed and I'm breathing hard. I don't have to look to know my clothes are in disarray, and my skin is hot everywhere. His eyes glitter hard as he rakes his gaze over me.

"Seduction isn't going to work, Scarlett, no matter how pretty your package. And I've meant everything I've said."

Like his threat. I haven't forgotten that. Of course I haven't. Promise, threat, call it what you will, we both know what it is. Exactly. And I'm playing with fire and my brother's future by playing Hudson.

Even if that's not my intent.

"I'm trying to help." The words are slightly breathless as I say them.

"By upping the ante?"

"Yes."

I'm still pressed against him and I know what I have to do.

He's not asking for me upping the ante like this. He knows we have that already. He's asking me for the truth.

I dig in.

I'm going to dive down into my white lies with more, pepper them carefully, so they don't seem as big as I think they're becoming, but I know I can get through all this. There isn't that much time and then after the meeting, after Hudson gets what he wants and he pays out, I spend the rest of the year rolling along until we split up.

What's a handful of lies and months between friends?

Not that we're friends, and I'm not under any illusions we'll be doing anything much except perhaps make appearances after he says he's in love and wants to marry me. They just want to see he's found a bride. It's not like he's inheriting a family fortune. He has his own. I just have to play my role and show him I'm trustworthy.

Dangerous games, I know, but I'm not out to hurt him or anyone.

I'm going to have to take him to my place in Brooklyn. And I know I discussed this with Amber, but what if she lets something slip?

That's if she's home.

But I have to do this. Take that risk.

And—

"Scarlett, you're plotting, I can see that." He sighs and releases me, then puts me from him and leans back in the seat. "I don't need plots. Just honesty."

"I know. And I'm going to give it to you."

He sits up and looks at me. "You are?"

"Yes."

"How?"

"I'll show you where I live." I pause. "In Brooklyn."

"When?" It's that dark note in his voice, like I'm playing for time that really does it.

And I look at him, and I smile. "How about now?"

Chapter Twenty-One

HUDSON

She's playing games. And I'm not sure why I'm going along with it.

Apart from that simple fact that if I'm going to do this, I don't have time to find someone else.

We head to Brooklyn.

I feel like a bullying ass, invading her life, pushing her to do this. Because, no matter how I set it up for her to think it was her choice, I pushed.

Thing is, I wouldn't care about her home if I still believed she lived back on Park. Maybe for the first time it's something I'm interested in, but that's not why.

I just need to know before I take the final step that I can trust her. If I put this out there, then there's no going back. And it's no longer the same as not taking up this challenge for the jewels if I fail. Because now, if I fail...

I'm not going to fail.

We don't talk as we cross the bridge and head into Bushwick. The edges of Bushwick? I didn't pay attention to what she told my driver, as I needed to send something out. It's getting late and I've got plans.

We arrive in an area that isn't money but close to the Halsey St L stop. This is the kind of area Magnus loves taking and turning on its head. That's not my area and I don't generally do much of Brooklyn outside certain parts such as Dumbo and even Park Slope.

The building is pre-war, the paint peeling and the trees old, along with some of the litter. But I noticed bars and restaurants in with the bodegas and old school supermarkets and dollar stores that tell me this place will be completely turned around in another five to ten years.

I give her a curious look as we pull up and disembark. Even for a rich girl with no money, this isn't a normal choice. I should ask Bixby about it, but then again, if she's out here, maybe she hasn't told anyone.

Who am I kidding? Of course she hasn't.

"This way," Scarlett says.

I'm imagining a place crammed full of expensive pieces that don't fit, and a closet that won't quit, but it's not that. When we climb the flight of stairs and she opens three locks with the kind of practiced ease that says to me she's lived here a while, we're in a lovely little apartment.

Emphasis on the little.

But it's cheery and looks good. Like she got someone in to make it hers.

"Oh!" A tall woman with the kind of curves Ryder would lose his mind over says as she steps out of the kitchen, a bottle of tequila in one hand. "Scarlett, I didn't expect a guest..."

Scarlett looks like she wants the floor to open and to swallow her whole. "This is my boss—"

"A little more than that," I find myself saying because suddenly I need to start the ball rolling and this seems as good a place as any to test it out.

The woman looks like she's going to say something, but she suddenly smiles and holds out her tequila-free hand. "Amber. Scarlett's roommate, and aren't you a dream?" She winks and hell yes, would Ryder be all over her. "I'm having a drink if you both want one, and then I'm out. Got a hot date."

"No thanks," Scarlett says, pushing me down the short hall from the living room, "we're not thirsty."

She pushes again and I'm so shocked I let her and then a door slams and I'm in a dark place that smells like Scarlett. Flowers bright and earthy and green and with a hint of sensual promises hidden. "You know what she's thinking."

Scarlett makes a sound that tells me she doesn't appreciate my dry humor. "You started it. You know, with the little bit more thing."

I move in close to her. Her presence surrounds me and then I have my arms around her, drawing her in and she's soft and perfect feeling. "Upping the ante. So, this is your place?"

"For now."

Her words are brittle and I swallow a laugh. Not at her place or what she feels is her predicament, but because she's all prickly when she doesn't need to be.

"So," I say, brushing my mouth against her ear, "does this place in here come with a light, or are you into bat living?"

"Do not mock me."

"I'm not."

"You are."

I slide my arm a little tighter around her. "Not on purpose, Scarlett. I'm sorry I got you to do this."

"My idea."

There's something strangely intimate about standing in her bedroom, holding her in the dark, while we're both completely dressed. I let her go and step back and she turns on a light.

There's a threadbare bear on the bed and everything in the room is in casual disarray and she sees me looking, rushing about, knocking things down while she tries to clean up. I just slide my hands in the pockets of my pants and wait.

Her roommate didn't know who I was, which is good. And not unexpected. I'm not sure she knows Scarlett's from money, which makes sense, I guess. Someone like Scarlett, who looks like she's been here a while, they don't talk about money issues. Old moneyed people never do, unless it's to impress. You're meant to know.

After all, that was drilled into me, too. But I prefer, like my brothers, making my own way.

My gaze keeps returning to the bear that's on the bed and I take the two steps across the worn floorboards to pick him up.

"Mr. Figglesmort," she blurts, snatching him from me and holding him.

"He was very safe with me."

She turns a delightful shade of dark rose. "He's just an old relic, that's all."

"Heirloom?"

"Something like that." Scarlett places him on the bed with a reverence I've only seen with expensive things from her type.

But then again, Scarlett keeps reinventing her own mold.

"You know," I say, "I'm not going to advertise you live here. Not that there's shame in it. I think that you taking me here was hard and you might think me knowing about this...where you live, makes things harder, but it makes it real. A lot more real than just cookie cutter representation."

Now I'm making an utter ass of myself and doing something I don't think I've done in years—screw up what I'm trying to say. I usually think it through, weigh it, find the right words, or hire the right people to say them for me. But here I am, spewing words at her that she just might take the wrong way.

I clear my throat and take hold of her shoulders. "All I wanted to say was I like you're not boring. You were never boring, but your home? I like it."

And even though I shouldn't, and because I can't think of anything to say beyond that, I kiss her.

It's just a kiss, a soft and sweet, fleeting kiss.

"Hudson, you should stop kissing me."

"Why? Do you want me to?"

"No, which is why yo u should."

She's got a point and I'm playing with fire and getting burned and it feels a little too good. But an idea's come to me, to go with my text earlier. I'm going to need to send some more, and really set the cat in among the pigeon. Get that ante up where I need it to be.

"Scarlett," I say, stepping back so I can breathe. "We're going out. And pack a bag. You're coming home with me."

"That's a terrible idea."

I frown. "I'm not asking for you to fuck me again. I have guest rooms. I think if we're upping the ante, we should do it right. For all intents and purposes. What do you say?"

"That it's a terrible idea."

"So is that a yes?"

She looks at me, those hazel eyes melting dark golden brown. "Yes."

We go to dinner at one of the hottest to be seen places across from the Park. The kind of place Ryder loves, Magnus wouldn't bother with, Kingston will use if he needs to, and that I abhor.

It's the place with a waiting list into next year and it's where those who want to be seen are, well, seen.

The food's decent.

I'm an attentive date, but Scarlett's easy to pay attention to. This doesn't seem to be her kind of place, but her eyes were wide when we stepped foot in here, so maybe it's a place she's wanted to go since it opened nine months ago. Who knows? I don't ask, she doesn't volunteer.

The dark red dress she wears that swirls a little around her calves is sexy in a way I wouldn't have thought about before. And when we leave, it's only natural to take her hand.

For the right reasons, obviously, but her hand feels good and warm and made to fit into mine.

I pull her into me and she comes willingly in the warm air of the night. She laughs and looks up at me. "You're good at this," she breathes.

I brush a strand of hair away from her face, lingering on her cheek that feels like satin beneath my fingertips. "Good at what?"

"Seduction? The perfect date? Whatever it is you're up to."

I brush my mouth against hers. "Upping the ante, Scarlett. Let's go get a nightcap."

"Okay."

It's not far to the upscale bar in red leather and black steel and oversized glasses of cocktails that need a real mixologist.

I know a lot of the people in the place, but they're the type to keep to themselves. I've slept with a number of women here too. They give Scarlett a once over before they turn to their latest goals, and she notices, but as we take our seat and place our drinks order, the jazz band's music at just the right tempo and level, I lean in and kiss her. This time, it's a deeper, more carnal kiss.

I meant for it to simply be a kiss for show, but it quickly gets away from me. Her response is like fire and she sets me ablaze.

"You keep complicating things," she whispers against my mouth.

I sample that mouth again, this time sliding my hand up under her skirt to rest against her naked thigh and wonder how far I can go. Here. In this place. "You make it very easy, Scarlett."

"The ante doesn't count if there's no one there to watch."

I laugh softly as I slide my hand a little higher and her fingers grip the edge of the table. "Is that like the tree thing in the woods?"

"No." And she lets go of the table and takes hold of my tie pulling me up against her and then her hand moves down, a deliberate ride, over my chest and torso, stopping just short of where my cock is stiffening in my pants. "You're teasing me. For reasons I don't understand."

"You're teasing me, Scarlett."

She smiles. "I'm getting back at you for doing that to me."

I push my hand higher, brushing at the juncture of her thighs.

I don't do this kind of thing. I don't take these risks in public, especially not with what I've gone and done. But she drives me to it. Somehow, someway, Scarlett makes things brighter, and she tests me, or makes me test myself. In short, with her, I very much do this kind of thing. And I like it.

"We can play this game, Scarlett," I say, "or we can go to my place and do it all for real."

"You want me."

"Of course I do. I thought that was obvious."

"Take me back to your place."

"Thank Christ," I say, "because we keep doing this and I'm going to end up embarrassed."

She laughs. "Maybe we should stay."

I pull her hand from my lap and withdraw mine from her leg and I kiss each and every one of her fingertips. "I think, Scarlett, we should go."

We barely make it in my front door before we're ripping at each other's clothing like we can't get enough. I know I can't. I don't know what she's done to me. It's the second night in a row that I'm caught in the fever of her.

There's no way we're going to make it up the stairs.

I drag her to the left, into the drawing room I keep for visitors, and I push her onto her stomach on the back of the sofa and flip the skirt of her dress up and over her.

The harsh sound of her breathing is a sexual pull against me and my cock is so hard it hurts.

Her ass in their black panties is a glorious thing.

"Spread your legs, Scarlett."

She does so with a small whimper as I slide my finger down along her panty covered slit. Hot and wet.

I can't wait. Not anymore.

"Hurry…"

Her word is fuel. And I fumble with the buttons on my fly and undo them and unleash my hard cock. I pump it in my hand, fisting it around the base, and then I'm there, pulling her panties to the side and those pink lips glisten, inviting me in and I'm not one to ignore such a delicious invitation.

Rubbing the head along her pussy, I line up and then I thrust in, and she cries out.

I bury myself to the hilt.

She's so tight and wet and she grips me, it's the most insanely pleasurable place to be, inside of her. And I stay like that, buried deep, for a long moment, breathing, trying to get myself down so I don't blow my load immediately.

And then I kiss her back. Kiss her nape, bite down as she moans low. "Please. Fuck me."

I do. I pump into her, in long, hard, deep strokes, each one a revelation. My entire body is singing and wound tight with need, and I can feel her tighten around me, even as my balls tighten and I'm not going to last.

She clamps down on me as her orgasm hits and she cries out. The contractions of her cunt on my cock are too strong, too much, and I come, too, deep, and it's a full on body explosion.

I rest my head against her nape, and brush it with my lips, savoring the salty sweetness of her skin, the slight dampness from our fucking.

"Hudson?"

"Yeah?" I'm still inside her, only half soft because I want her again.

"That was just a starter, right?"

And I laugh.

A man, if he believed in love, could fall for this woman, I think.

"Try and stop me from doing all that again."

And I reluctantly pull out of her, and take her up the stairs, a slow, meandering walk up the floors with plenty of interesting stops and loss of clothes along the way, and we do it all again.

All night long.

I'm not used to leaving someone at my place when I head to work.

I'm not used to having overnight guests on the whole and I never have them on my private floor.

Still, there's something about Scarlett... It doesn't really matter, I tell myself as I head out after a trip to my gym in the house. It's not even six am, but I have a lot to do and the things I put in motion, well, I need to check on those.

Everything's running smoothly to my satisfaction and Scarlett comes to work on time, no doubt facing the small wall of work I left her.

It's almost lunchtime when there's a harried knock on my door and it bursts open.

Scarlett stands there, in charcoal trousers and a cream shirt that looks good, but it's her face that has my attention.

She's pale, eyes wide, looking nervous.

"What is it?"

"It wasn't me. I don't...I don't know how..." She moves quickly to my desk and holds out her phone, shaking it in front of me. "Oh, God."

She's worked up, in a tizzy as my mother used to say, and the phone is moving so much I can't see what she's trying to show me before the screen goes black.

"Scarlett, use your words."

"You and me. We're on social media. As a couple. I don't know how that happened." She pulled the phone back to her and pressed it, then put it in front of me. "See." She shoved a finger at it.

Shit. "Scarlett—"

"Photos. Of you and me."

I start to rise. "Scarlett, you—"

"It wasn't me. I'm sorry! It's somehow out there. Please don't fire me."

Chapter Twenty-Two

SCARLETT

I'm freaking out. I know this and I can't stop. The sun beats down on me through the window, pummeling into me, it feels like. I know it isn't doing that. But I can't shake that hot seat, spotlight feeling and it isn't helping by Hudson rising to his feet, and coming around to face me.

My breath comes short and fast and not just from fear. He rounds the desk and comes up to me, hands large and warm and firm as he takes hold of my upper arms.

"It had to be last night. We shouldn't have…I know you want to keep everything as much on the downlow or a needs to know level, even with upping the ante. You hate the media, and it's there. And I'm there."

Mystery woman.

What even is that?

There's a part of me that wants it to shout my name, but why would they? I'm nobody. Worse, if they did, what a can of worms. Already my heart is jumping because what if his friend, Sarah's cousin, sees it?

They're not close, I know that. Not Sarah and Bixby, and not Bixby and Hudson. Not to mention this is in New York based gossip pages.

But we live in a global community, one that loves getting in other people's business.

I swallow hard, my skin alive and blood hot in my veins at Hudson's touch. And I remember everything we did last night. In the living room downstairs, on all those stairs, against his floor's wall, the bed...

With great effort, I push that all away. I'd rather not, it's way more pleasant than thinking about the pictures and the little article.

It's all out of hand. Things are out there. He'll blame me. He'll find out the truth. Then he'll come for me and my brother. And—

"Scarlett?"

I blink. He's not morphing into a wrathful creature from hell. He's not angry. His dark blue gaze is warm, not full of fire. There's not even a hint of brimstone. Hudson's mouth turns up in the slightest of smiles and I stare up at him.

"Yes?"

"Oh, good, you're back."

"I was thinking of escaping to the ether, but you've tethered me down by your manhandling."

Hudson laughs. Actually, for real, laughs. I'm not shocked because it's at my feeble joke or that he can do that. I know he can. It's the fact he's doing it now.

"This isn't manhandling," he says, the tone light. "Now, have you calmed?"

"A smidge. Why are you so calm? Did you break your brain?"

He lets me go and leans back against his desk, crossing his arms over his chest. He's not wearing his jacket, just the dove gray shirt and slate gray vest and trousers. And as he crosses his ankles, I catch a flash of an emerald-green sock. The man has hidden and unexpected depths. But I knew that.

"No. I've been trying to tell you something."

Alarm bells start ringing somewhere from inside me. I narrow my eyes. "What?"

"I set it up."

For a moment I don't move.

Time has stopped or I've gone and done it, finally lost my mind. Because it sounded like Hudson just told me he'd done something he'd never do. He—he did say that.

I replay it again, just to be sure.

Nope, definitely.

I narrow my eyes. "You did what now?"

"Set it up." He uncrosses his arms and spreads them wide.

"Why would you do that? They made it sound like I was some dirty secret! Mystery woman?"

The corner of his mouth twitches and it sets my blood boiling. Oh, yeah, it bubbles and spits in my veins and it takes everything I am not to shove him. Hard.

"I upped the ante. That's why we went to those places, especially the dinner. Come on, you know I'm not the type to go there."

He wasn't and it hadn't even hit me. I was just so caught up in him after pulling off showing him my place, so impressed he didn't wrinkle his nose or look down on me or judge me as the fallen rich girl. He doesn't know that's just me and my place and I've never been rich, but he didn't judge me for what he thinks I am and that meant something.

Like me being an idiot, obviously.

"So you took me out to...what? Get a photo-op and a fuck?"

He winces. "The first, yes, the second wasn't a plan. That happened."

"And gullible Scarlett went for it." I shake my head, not sure who I'm more disgusted with, him or me.

Him because he's pissing me off, and me because...yes, I wanted to sleep with him, I still do...I went there again thinking, I don't know what. Not that we'd suddenly get a happy ending. This man doesn't believe in the romantic happy ending. I'm sure one day he'll decide to pick someone suited to him and his life and position her just so and honestly, I hope he's really miserable in the little hypothetical I just conjured.

And— I'm off topic. I'm pissed off. I'm furious. I want to make him bleed. And cry. Although I don't think he does the latter.

Shit. Why am I so mad?

"We talked about upping the ante. I made a decision. Give a little whiff of a scandal to push things forward. I'm not sure why you're upset about the sex."

I sniff. "I'm not."

He just looks at me like I'm lying. Which I am. And it makes me even madder. "The sex, we agreed, was a separate entity, just sex. You—"

"I'm not. I just don't like the feeling of being used."

"I'm paying you."

It's the reason in his tone that makes me stalk up to him and shove him. "I'm not your property. This is a fake relationship. Not just sort of fake boss and sort of fake employee."

"Scarlett, you're complicating things. I just wanted a nice, well-bred woman who needed extra cash from the same social strata as me. I figured you would take the money, and like any good girl of good breeding, you wouldn't talk about your failed relationships."

"I'm also not a horse."

"No. Horses have a better temperament. Even the difficult ones."

"You, Hudson, are a complete asshole."

"And you're being a class A brat. Stop it."

"Make me."

His gaze crashes with mine and I can barely breathe as the heat of that loaded, bone-melting tension rises between us. "Is that," he asks softly, "a challenge?"

"No." Oh, is that word hard to say. "You said scandal. What are you trying to turn me into?"

"My pretend wife to be. Come on, you're working for me. I don't go around fucking the help. So, upping the ante with a whiff of a scandal is perfect. It all goes together. It was basically your idea."

My head is spinning, but I think it's because we're so close and that fire in his gaze is sexual and predatory and I'm the kind of victim who's tying herself to the rock.

The tricky thing is I know Sarah well enough to know she'd go with the flow. She'd probably try to marry him because he's almost the whole package, and would be complete and perfect if he had a heart he wanted to use. Which he doesn't. Which wouldn't stop her.

I don't want to marry him and we're both using each other, and we agreed sex was just sex and still I'm furious and I don't understand why.

"I think," I snap, "I have to go."

Whipping around, I take a step towards the door, but he can move fast. He's right there, my wrist caught in his hand as he pulls me back to face him.

He stares down at me with narrowed eyes that still burn with fire, but it's a mix of anger and sex and it turns me on more than it has any right to. "Where the fuck do you think you're going?"

"Away."

"I haven't said you can leave."

I move into him, brushing my body against him, and it's like brushing against an exposed low-current live wire. A buzz and a thrill and a charge. "I don't need your permission."

"There are several pieces of paper with your signature on it, Scarlett, that says I can. There's the fact if you go and walk out the door and screw this up, I'll screw up things for you."

Placing my palm flat on his chest I go to push him, but he clamps his other hand on my wrist, holding me, and I'm trapped. Caught by him. Literally and figuratively. Because the way he looks at me, like I'm dessert that might be laced with poison but he's damn hungry anyway, holds me there more than the physical.

I couldn't walk away even if I tried.

"Hudson, I just want to get away for a bit. Calm down."

"No."

"No?" Heat and need is pooling in my body, and even though he's been in it, even though we had sex a few hours ago, I start to ache for him all over again. I crave him.

"That's what I said."

"Why?"

He lets me go, only to twine his arms around me and draw me in and he stops, mouth a breath from mine he says, "This."

And Hudson kisses me. It's like an explosion of need as our mouths meet and open. Tongues dance and tease and duel. The carnal power rocks me right down through my core, right into the marrow of my bones.

I kiss him back and it's not enough. How is it never enough?

He spins me, his hands everywhere, in my hair, skimming my body, sliding up between my thighs as I hit the desk.

I open for him and he steps in, his hand there, on my pussy, and I feel it through the layers of the material and he strokes and pushes against me with his fingers, teasing my clit with little light squeezes that are just sharp enough to send jolts of an almost-orgasm through me. I reach for him, for his fly, and his hand rises up to my zipper.

I'm ready, I'm so ready for this, here, now.

And then he's there, my zipper is a hiss in the air and I raise my hips, and bite down on his throat as he reaches in.

I'm going to reach my own personal nirvana in seconds, all I need is him to touch my bare, wet flesh—

"Knock knock?" Someone says.

And we both freeze.

Chapter Twenty-Three

HUDSON

I don't know whether to kill my fucking brother or quietly hand him some kind of award for stopping me doing something absolutely insane in my office.

"Don't let me stop you, kids," Ryder says cheerfully. "I'm not one to stop fun and games—"

"If you want to keep breathing, shut the fuck up," I say pleasantly, something which I'm very far from feeling.

Scarlett's head is buried against my shoulder and she's gone stiff in my arms. At least my brother's timing has killed both the mood and my boner, and I resolutely zip her pants up for her and smooth a hand over her hair.

I want to reassure her, which is a little surprising. I don't tend to need to, and I didn't think I'd ever want to do something like that, but she brings something out in me I'm not sure I'm a fan of.

And of course she needs a moment or two to get it together. That escalated fast and it hadn't been on my agenda. On my mind, yes. The sex is that good with her. It's the kind of sex where I want to spend a week naked with her and do all sorts of depraved things.

She gives me a little push and I release her and turn to face my brother, who's craning his neck to see her. He's such an idiot.

"We're both dressed. I'll buy you some porn for your birthday if you're that hard up."

"Does anyone buy porn these days?" Ryder asks, not upset at all.

I fold my arms. "I don't know. I don't have your problem."

"I don't have that particular problem, either." Ryder suddenly grins as Scarlett steps out around me to my side.

I glance at her and she's flushed red, and her hair is mussed. Lips swollen and— She looks exactly like what we've been doing. I probably don't look any better, either.

Part of me wishes it had been Jenson who'd walked in and not my brother. But part of me, a bigger part, wishes no one had. I'm not ashamed to admit I'm more than interested in seeing which delicious way this would have gone.

"At least it's Scarlett."

She frowns. "Of course it's me." Then her eyes go big. "I didn't mean. I mean, I did. I just—"

Scarlett goes quiet and I look at my brother. "Did you find anything more?"

"A lot." He pulls a newspaper from under his arm. An actual newspaper. "You're online, too. It's not much. You're not me, but because we're related, here you are, larger than life. When I say larger, I mean in print."

"I set it up. It's small and you know it." I tap my fingers against my desk as I ease back against it. This seems safer, putting a little distance between me and Scarlett, because I really want to touch her, comfort her.

Not that she needs comforting. Maybe the word is soothe. Or maybe I just want to fucking touch her.

I should have gone out and gotten laid before this all started. I should have gone and found a willing woman—and there were a lot—instead of touching Scarlett.

But none of them have hair that color of dark honey. Or that weird and quirky sense of humor. Or her ability to say the most outrageous thing.

And I bet none of them own what looks like a rat-bit old bear with the name of Mr. Figglesmort.

"You?" He shakes his head and glances at Scarlett. "What have you done to my brother?"

"He's done it all himself. He's like a martini—"

"You came here to gossip?" I ask, cutting her off.

But Ryder's interest is piqued. "He's a martini? What am I? Something outrageously seductive and naughty. I figure—"

"Ryder, I'm busy, and I thought you were, too."

"I took some time out of my day to give you the heads up." He wanders over to the window and stares out over Manhattan, then leans his shoulder against the glass and rolls towards me with a sigh. "I've seen it. King and Mag have, too. But I'm here because it seems everyone has."

My mind starts burning new pathways.

This is good. I'm embarrassed, so is Scarlett, and Ryder can't help himself with gossip. He loves it. I can use this. I can spin this a little tighter. Tell him this started one way and ended up something more...

I turn to Scarlett and push away from the table, taking the small step towards her, and that pull starts in earnest all over again. She has power, this woman. I've thought it before, and here I am thinking it again: I can use that.

Smoothing her hair, I kiss her softly and for a brief moment she stiffens and then her lips cling to mine.

Christ they're soft and so unbelievably morish. I pull back. "I need to talk to Ryder about this. Seeing as it's now out there. Take the afternoon off."

She's about to argue, but she suddenly closes her mouth. "Okay. We'll continue this soon," she says, and then Scarlett turns, gives my brother a small wave and rushes out.

Ryder studies me. "Well, that was interesting."

"That's one way of putting it," I say, moving back around my desk as I start to tidy up, getting things ready for the afternoon.

I'm ready, but this gives me something to do.

"Things look like they've taken a...turn."

"Yes."

It's not lying. Exactly. I'm leading him in the direction he's thinking. He's putting things together all on his own. And this is going to help. Ryder will sell it because he believes it.

Not that he wouldn't before, but an added layer of authenticity helps.

"That's good."

"Yes, it is." I flick through open tabs on my computer and suddenly I stop and look up.

Good?

"What do you mean?"

Ryder shrugs and comes over to me and leans on the desk. "I'm not here to gossip about your newly found love, Hud."

I almost correct him but stop myself. "Explain this to me, please."

He grins, and it's his shit-eating grin that got him beaten up a lot by us as a kid.

"Well," he says, expansively, "I told you already. People have seen it."

"Yeah, not just our brothers. Everyone."

Something drips down my spine, like a cold excitement, spreading out in waves as it pools at the base of my spine. "Like who?"

"Jenson." He pauses. "Mother."

"That's...good. That's really good. I mean I was trying to think of a way to up the ante here. Help prove the authenticity."

He raises a brow and laughs. "Do what I walked in on you doing and I think you've got yourself some down-home authenticity, Hudson."

"I'm not fucking someone in public."

"Pity." He sighs. "It's a thrill ride."

"I'm..." I run a hand over my hair. "I just need for all this to work. And the more proof I have, the better."

"Yeah, well, I spoke to Mother, and she's loving this."

"Of course she is. That woman can't wait for one of us to fall." I can't help the bitterness in my tone.

I don't know why she's wanting that. Her love life has been a disaster.

"And you're the first. Take notes."

"I'm not—" I stop, glare at him. "What do you mean 'take notes'?"

"As I said. I spoke to her. She's excited by all this. She's probably already planning a white wedding the likes of which Manhattan hasn't seen in decades."

"For fuck's sake. She can go and unplan that."

"Yeah?" Ryder straightens up and stretches, cricking his neck. "Well, you can tell her yourself. Or, rather, get your bride to be to do it."

"What do you mean?"

"Yes," says a voice from the doorway, and I turn. Scarlett's standing there, her gaze worried. "What do you mean?"

Ryder turns to her, then looks from me to her and back again. "Mother wants to meet you."

"She has." Both Scarlett and I say it at the same time, which makes Ryder's smile grow bigger.

"Not," he says, "formally."

"Oh, God."

Scarlett comes over. "What do you mean, formally, and why oh God?"

"Because..." I take her shoulders and I'm not sure whether it's to steady her or myself, "she wants an official one on one with you."

"Wh-when?"

And Ryder clicks his fingers and points at her. "I knew I didn't want you to leave, pretty Scarlett. Mother's planning a meeting in..." He checks his phone. "Twenty minutes."

Chapter Twenty-Four

SCARLETT

Twenty minutes?

This is insane. Now I'm meeting his mother?

I mean, I've met her, I've talked to her, but this is different. This is an interview for the job of daughter-in-law and I'm panicking hard like I'm actually up for it. Not that getting married is a job.

Or maybe it is. Maybe Hudson's such a mama's boy all the ladies have to pass the test. But the moment the thought springs to life in my head, I dismiss it. He's definitely not that, and I highly doubt any of his brothers are.

Maybe this is how things are done in his world.

Thing is, there isn't a handbook on it. And I could text Sarah and hope like hell she responds, but then I'd have to tell her everything and I can't.

I wait to see if I'm going to faint, but I'm not. I've never fainted in my life and clearly, I'm not about to start doing so now. Worst luck.

"Are you alright?" Hudson says, all velvet voiced.

"You look pale."

"Go away, Ryder, I've got this," Hudson says to his brother.

"I'm fine." I take a breath and try to smile. "See?"

"Well, as much as I'd love to stay and see how this all plays out, I've got a meeting to get to." Ryder looks seriously disappointed.

And Hudson looks like he wants to kill him. In this, I might be on Hudson's side. Because right now, I feel a little like an attraction at a circus sideshow.

"She'll be calling you, but I figured I'd give you the heads up."

"Thanks," Hudson says, not looking anywhere near as perturbed by this as I am. "I don't have anything else from Jenson."

"Yeah, I know how that feels. Guess we'll find out when this goes through." His brother puts his phone away. "And at least we know what's riding on it."

That doesn't make me feel any better.

Ryder starts to head to the door and stops. "Twenty minutes, at The Park."

That's an old school, famous brasserie that old moneyed New York love. It's gorgeous, it's art-deco because that's the era when it was built, and it's expensive as hell.

I'm in my work clothes.

Inside me the panic and a new round of fury whip themselves into a frenzy.

The moment his brother leaves I turn on him.

Hudson raises an eyebrow. "Shouldn't you go get ready?"

I start ticking things off on my left hand. "One, I just found out. Two, you're damn lucky I came back to see if you wanted me to email the Meyer group before I left since apparently, they're important. Three, I live in Brooklyn. I can't get home and back in twenty minutes. Four, The Park? I'm not dressed for The Park. That's five. And it brings us back to three." I start on the right hand. "Six, why do I have to meet your damn mother again, anyway? Seven, this isn't in the contract. Eight—"

"Stop, I get it. This is a lot." He says it in a way that tells me he doesn't think so, that tells me he's thinking I'm overreacting.

And that sets the anger boiling and spitting.

I glare at Hudson. "No. You don't get it. That can be nine through to a million—"

"Hey." He grabs my hands in his. They're warm and they make me fuzzy about the edges and then I remember what we were doing and I try to pull them free but Hudson doesn't release me. "Scarlett, stop being a baby."

Oh. God. This man knows the exact buttons he shouldn't push. I hate him. Violently.

"I'm not. You're the mama's boy."

He laughs. "I'm a what?" His thumb moves slowly against my skin, sending shivers through that spitting, boiling, wild anger. I'm a complete firestorm and his touch is heaven.

And I'm not having it.

"You apparently can't do anything without her. And why do I have to go alone?" I should pull free, move away. I should—

"She wants to see you, Scarlett."

"So she asks and you jump?" I spit the words at him.

They bounce away from his sudden Teflon surface. "Technically that's you and, come on, you know the deal."

Those low, calming, velvety tones are not what I need, even as I want to sink down into them. And he's cooling the anger because he won't stop that sinuous slide of his thumb against my skin. I swallow. "It's not to meet your mother."

Hudson's eyes narrow a little. "I didn't plan this."

His phone starts ringing at that moment and that only sparks my anger again. "You call her mother."

"She's not the mom type," he says, moving a little closer to me, ignoring the ring of the phone on his desk behind him. "Only when we're pissed off. You know the drill."

I don't. Our grandparents bought us up. No big deal for me and Danny, it was normal, but he's talking opulence and moneyed lifestyles and that I am not familiar with. "Of course, but I didn't expect—"

"Jenson put her up to this, I'll bet anything," he mutters. "Or it's to do with my father's fucking will."

"See? Mama's boy."

He laughs, but his eyes are deadly serious. "Not at all, Scarlett. But there are games we need to play to do this, and you should know that."

"Not unexpected ones," I say.

"Why the fuck do you think I'm paying you so much?"

It hurts, those words. And I don't know why.

"To keep quiet," I snap.

His mouth hardens. And his thumb stops working its magic against my skin and he lets me go, stepping back a little and that hurts worst of all. It's like I've slammed shut a door without knowing it. And I don't know what to do.

"Fine, I'll pay you a bonus." He tilts his head a little, blue eyes glittering darkly. "Happy now?"

"Not at all, Hudson."

He pinches the bridge of his nose with his fingers. "Just... just go and do it. Please. I'll make sure you get the bonus. And work clothes are fine."

"Did I cross some kind of Hudson line?" Sarcasm drips from my voice.

"No. Simply sticking to the rules of the letter. I'll send the lawyer a note to add a bonus for you." He moves away from me, back around his desk and he sits down, pulling his computer to him and I know I've been dismissed.

I don't move.

He looks up. "That all, Scarlett?"

We stare at each other and it's clear he's not happy with me either and I don't know how we spiraled to here.

Without a word, I turn and leave, and go and make myself presentable. There's only the staff bathroom but I head down to another floor to use one of those. I might be his PA to everyone else, but the perks don't extend to my own bathroom, and even if they did, I don't want to swan out looking ready for the world in front of people here who know me. The other floors aren't in the day-to-day world of Hudson, so...

I stare at my face in the mirror of the beautiful bathroom, all sleekly modern with a flower arrangement in one corner of the slate gray marble counter and practice a smile. Then I stop, because I've met his mother and I get the uncomfortable feeling she can spot a fake a mile away.

Instead, I tie and pin my hair back in what I hope approximates a cool and elegant low bun.

Scrounging in my fake Coach bag—rather, Amber's fake Coach bag—I pull out eyeliner and mascara and touch up. It's not really my thing, but a little won't hurt. And then I dig for lipstick, but I stare at it in horror.

I wear a matte gloss mostly. That's not in here. Siren red, which must be Amber's, does not in any way at all say classy girl who knows the Hamptons.

With a shudder, I drop the tube in gold casing back in the bag and bite my lips like a baby vampire with no idea.

And then with a deep breath, I'm out of there. I'm running out of time. My phone buzzes and I glance at it as I head out of the bathrooms and into the hall towards the elevator. Martini, because of course Hudson can't trust me on this. I shove the phone back in my bag and go to face the mother lion.

I'm a mess of nerves as I step into the wide, cool, and expensive place. There are floor to ceiling glass windows, tables with crisp linen, and beautiful pale green seats in a lush material. There are plants, for crying out loud. The fixtures are brass, the lighting low, the wallpaper of subtle vines in raised gold and cream and white to die for, and the gleaming red floorboards look like you could slide on happily.

It's all meant to project calm and I feel anything but. I'm hot. I'm sweaty from my run here, and I look out of place in my not at all designer clothes and knock off bag.

I almost turn and scurry out the door when a waiter in black and an elegant black apron to finish his whole waiter goth vibe smiles and tells me politely to follow him.

Shit. She's seen me. Sent someone to fetch me. I swallow down some cool air laden with delicious scents that make my stomach growl.

I don't know why I'm in such a terrible panic. I've been on such a roller-coaster of emotions today and this shouldn't matter beyond just speaking when spoken to and pushing through.

After all, his mother isn't the one who's making this whole decision on whether to believe Hudson, and how did it get to be so big and complicated with everything riding on one small little job I took for money?

I follow the waiter into a darker, quieter corner of the restaurant, and she's there, looking at me, and it's like someone grabs my heart and squeezes.

She looks like Hudson in that moment. Well, I know, she's his mother, but it's not that resemblance, it's something in her expression.

Martini.

That's what it is.

And everything tumbles over me. My stomach lurches and I want to go throw up. Because I think I know why I'm such a mess around Hudson recently. Why I'm so angry and yet his touch can melt everything. It's him. I like him.

I like him a lot.

Oh. Fuck. I might be in love with him.

I'm in freefall at that, and from somewhere I hear a voice.

"Scarlett?"

I almost stumble into the seat the waiter is holding for me. It's either that or run. I sort of fall into a heap in the chair and I can't find my smile. "That's me, Mrs—" I stop.

I've forgotten her name. Does she go by her first, which I can't for the life of me remember, or by Sinclair or by something else?

She sits, a study in pure smooth martini with bite, and she's probably a pink gin martini with a perfect cocktail onion.

Why the hell am I on about martinis again?

"I forgot your name." The words blurt from me. "I was going to say Mrs. Sinclair, but then I couldn't remember—"

She smiles, places one smooth, cool hand on mine. "Call me Faye." Her hand lifts and returns to her lap. "So, you and Hudson?"

"Yes. It's weird."

Did I just say that out loud?

"Weird?"

I did. "I mean, him, me, but you know what they say!" The waiter is back and I look at him. "Martini. Up. Vodka. Six olives."

They're on my brain. I might as well embrace them.

A delicate eyebrow raises and Faye says, "I was concerned since you're working for him."

"I'm not planning to forever."

"Once you're married I imagine you'd like to get more involved in charity?"

"God no." I'm horrified. I had meant to just murmur nice things and keep it all sweet and bland.

"Really? Your own business?" She pauses. "You said something about computers when we first met."

I need to veer her into safer pastures like the weather or Fashion Week or Vogue or something. "Artificial intelligence. That's my passion, in regards to a career."

"And Hudson is fine with it?"

"Hudson." My hands fist and all common sense flies out the window. "Can jump in a lake if he thinks women should stay at home or do lady jobs. I don't even know what a lady job is. Although, even though I'm mad at him, he's not really the type to tell a woman what to do for a living."

"He's rich. You don't have to do anything for a living."

I narrow my eyes, forgetting I'm meant to be Sarah, and I say, "I'm not out to catch a rich man. And if I was, I'm sure there must be easier ones."

My words slap me in the face. Did I just say that to his mother?

"You, Scarlett, are a handful for him. So, tell me about this career."

And it just goes downhill from there.

Most of the time with Faye passes in a nightmarish blur. I keep putting my foot in it. I told her I'm not into fancy restaurants or the latest fashions. I did bring up Fashion Week, but when she pressed me about my favorite runway houses, I panicked.

It was more than obvious I'm not really into all the things Sarah was brought up to be, or at least be good at.

Falling in love with Hudson, that's easy. Way too easy.

But having to pretend that to his mother when I do? It's too much, and I failed.

Now what am I going to do?

There's only one week left before everything just might come crumbling down in that stupid test sprung on us and what that means to Hudson. And what failure means to me and therefore Danny if, well, I can't pass.

What if in that test they find out I'm not some rich girl? What if that's how Hudson finds out the truth? Even if I do love him, I may as well not because there is no future for us. There wasn't before and there certainly won't be if we pass this thing or fail.

No future, regardless of him knowing the truth or not.

And if I thought I could pull it off and have him get everything he wanted and the payout for Danny, I'd just do it, but after that...I'm not too sure.

I don't want him to lose those things he wants.

So what the hell do I do?
There's nothing to do.
Except tell him.

Chapter Twenty-Five

HUDSON

Scarlett is waiting for me on my doorstep when I get home that evening.

I stop as I reach her, and she rises to her feet. It's already dark out, but New York always shines, and between the streetlamp on the curb near my home on its old, tree lined strip and the soft light from my outside light I can see her perfectly.

She takes my breath, she really does. Her dark honey hair is beautiful always, but in this light, it's spectacular, and the way she defiantly lifts her chin is something I can feel down in my bones.

I unlock my door and the smart lights bloom as I gesture inside.

For a moment, Scarlett hesitates, something darkening the light of her hazel eyes. Maybe it's the makeup. It's slight, but she usually wears none. I don't even know why I notice.

"She liked you," I say, putting her out of her misery, because I decide that's what it is.

Scarlett steps inside but doesn't speak, just closes the door and hugs herself.

"My mother, that is," I clarify. "She liked you before, but this time she wanted to have a real one on one, and I don't know what you said or did, but she told me she thinks you're a perfect match for me. I've no idea what that means in all this, if anything, but well done."

Scarlett moves then, reaching for me and grabbing me and pulling me to her. And then she rises up and kisses me. A shock, like an electric current, runs through me from that contact.

It's not just the kiss, it's the fact she does it. The touch of her lips on mine isn't light. It isn't overtly sexual. It's something else I can't put my finger on, something that tastes a little bittersweet, and then I stop thinking as the kiss changes, morphs into passion.

And I'm there for it. Seems I always am with her. She smells like those flowers and morning dew. Clean, not too sweet, yet somehow evocative and seductive and it slides through me, warming me.

Or maybe it's her. I wrap my arms around her and pull her flush against me, our mouths opening and our tongues dancing slow and sensual and I'm hard and ready to fuck her then and there.

Then again, I could hold off on that pleasure, because kissing her is delicious. That heat and wetness and Scarlett taste that sometimes invades my dreams.

And here, where there's no one to witness such a slow, melting kiss, one that isn't foreplay but could be, the foreplay without the urgency, it feels natural. Like this is something I want to do with her because I can.

Like it could be leading into hot sex or it could just be a kiss all on its own. Both merited, both perfection.

Scarlett breaks the kiss and leans her forehead against my chest. I can feel the hammering of her heart as I hold her. The little harsh intakes of air as she steadies herself are something I understand. And want.

It's a little shocking, to have this feel so good and right and part of life.

Kissing isn't like that for me. Hasn't been since I was a hormone fueled teen. But with Scarlett...yeah, with her apparently it is.

And I like it.

Probably because this has a shelf life. Probably because it isn't real, no matter how real it might feel in the moment. I pull myself back into that headspace, the familiar one that has a well-worn groove I know.

Scarlett lifts her head and I smooth my hand over it, lingering a moment at her nape, against the warm and delicate skin there, beneath the softness of her hair.

"We need to talk," she says.

"You're right."

And she is. Because this thing between us is good and something I can use, I appreciate her honesty, as unwieldy and left of center as it might sometimes be, I can also give back.

I'm not being entirely truthful. Giving back, yes, but I also want her to understand the depth of meaning all this has taken on for me. The family jewels and the company.

"Um, okay." Scarlett pulls free and wipes her hands down her thighs. She looks around, trying to see where to sit.

But I stop her with a hand placed gently on her shoulder. "I'll go first."

I want to go upstairs to my private floor. Instead, I lead her from the wide hall and into the front living room. It's comfortable and I sometimes work down here. The view from the window is weirdly a lovely snapshot of New York that reminds me of yesteryear. My quiet street helps, as does the large magnolia tree outside that twists and turns in the narrow space between window and iron fence and pavement beyond on the street.

We did have sex in here, and for a moment I get a flash of us fucking all over the house. We haven't done that, but I'd like to.

I sit in the leather armchair and cross my legs, tapping my fingers against the arms. What the hell does that mean, anyway?

Scarlett perches on the sofa's corner and places her hands on her thighs, like she's ready to run.

She's like that. A complete and utter mess of contradictions.

It really strikes hard, hits home that she means a hell of a lot to me. More than I'd ever thought she would, and I'm not sure what that even means, or how she means so much. But she does. And I want to give her something because I know I owe her.

"Scarlett, time's running out, I get that. But that's not what I want to say. I guess I want to say thank you."

"To me?"

I laugh at the disbelief in her voice and smile. "Yeah, to you. There are so many ways this could have gone, but you…you've surpassed everything for me in the authenticity. So I want to give back, be honest with you."

"Oh, God. You have a secret family, don't you? A secret life. Maybe—"

"I do not have a family other than the one you've met." I shudder at the thought of being trapped by the fakeness we're sold as love, even if someone like Scarlett could definitely convince any other man it actually exists.

"Oh."

"This is important to me."

She nodded. "I'm not saying family jewels, because…but yeah, I get it."

I half smile at that. "No, you don't. I'm rich. I don't need to point that out, but this isn't about power or money. It's, for me, legacy. Growing up, the legend, the myth of the Sinclair jewels were instilled in us. People have tried to find them. They've been written about. Arguments have been made over the decades whether they're real or if they aren't, how much they're worth… and then I grew up. Made my own money and stopped thinking about them."

"You don't need to tell me any of this."

"I know," I say, looking at her, "not in that way, but I need to. And you're different, Scarlett. I don't get how or why, but you're unlike anyone I've met. This thing is bigger than what you signed on for."

That feels like better footing. The rest seems to skate close to a nest of emotions I'm not sure I want to visit. I look at the perfect crease in my suit pants, at the shine on my shoes, and for once I'm a little sick of all that. Maybe her rough edges that I like are contagious.

"And because it's bigger you should know why you're giving up a longer period of your life to this thing I'm doing." I blow out a breath. My house is too quiet. It needs life and sound and laughter and the sorts of things someone like Scarlett can breathe into it. I push that thought away with everything else and focus on my words.

"It's not money or power. It's about something more important. Family legacy and what it means to me. Having the proof they exist is like having a connection to history, a piece of the family. And…even my father.

"Some say, me included, that the old man was all about money and power and the company and they wouldn't be wrong. I grew up with the man. Business was always set higher than anything else for him. But if my father did this, it's a way, proof I guess is one way of putting it...it shows he did really care about me. And that means everything. I want one of those supposedly lost to time jewels because it's something tangible. A connection."

For a long moment she doesn't say a word. And then she speaks.

"Love of family," she says softly. "I get it. We all go to great lengths for that."

"It's just having a piece means the world. I didn't expect to lose a piece of the flagship company if I fail. And that..." I shrug, "I don't deal with it day to day or anything, but it's in private hands—the Sinclair hands—with a small part public, and that's legacy, too. But if I lose my part if this thing goes under, I...I won't be happy, but it stays in the family. I just don't have my shares, but I'm sure I can buy them back."

I'm not sure who I'm trying to convince, or why I'm babbling at her.

But I do know.

"It means everything to me, Scarlett," I say, finally letting the words out. "Everything."

"I get that, and you—"

"No, Scarlett." I get to my feet and start to pace because this is an area I don't go. "I've told you that. But thing is, it means everything to me that you're doing this."

"Oh." Her gaze skittered over me as she smoothed her hands against her thighs once more. Long, slender thighs.

And it comes on me then, what it is I really want to say. This isn't something I do lightly, or often, or...ever if I'm honest, but...

I stop and look at her. "Scarlett, thing is, I wanted you to know that because I do get what things are worth. I work a lot. I don't believe in love, but it does mean everything to me. And I know the next part with this interview might be difficult. I think, though, we can do it. Because I really like you."

She staring at me like I've grown two heads and there's something in her gaze, something complicated that's like heat and darkness and light and hope and despair. I'm reading into things, I know.

"The attraction is real, the one I have for you. And after this...who knows, maybe we can still see each other." I've commandeered the conversation, I realize. I look at her.

"What was it you wanted to say?"

Chapter Twenty-Six

SCARLETT

Oh. My. God.

I do not, at all, know what to say.

I'm pretty sure good intentions have packed up and left. I think they did that somewhere between him explaining what this all means to him and that he's attracted to me and wants to see me.

Anyone else, that's nothing.

In Hudson land, I get the feeling all his words mean something much bigger.

And here I am, in a luxe and tasteful living room, the one where we had hard and mind blowing sex, a room that suddenly feels more like a rock and a hard place or a fire and frying pan. Or whatever cliché it is I'm suddenly caught in. Because of my little white lie that grew legs.

I have big, out-of-control feelings for him. The big L word. And the more I listened, the more I fell for him. Because I got what he was trying to say.

The reason he's doing all this isn't to get his hands on a prize he can't buy, it's out of a sense of family and belonging, and to him it's a piece of the love his father probably never expressed.

He's doing this because he's human. He might be the hottest thing I've seen, and a bordering on perfect specimen of a man. He's definitely richer than I can imagine. But he's willing to do anything for that family connection.

And me? I'm in this for money on the surface, but that money's to save my brother from perhaps trusting someone else carelessly, but Danny didn't deserve to be where he is, languishing on the bottom. Not with debts he can't pay, debts that aren't his, and not with a big fat black ball with his name on it, courtesy of his ex partner.

I go to tell Hudson the truth.

"You know what?"

His mouth lifts a little. "It depends if I'm going to like what you say."

"It's all going to be okay. I'll fix this for you. Not that anything needs fixing. I mean, I'll make sure we make this happen, but—"

A bright ringing sound rushes through the house. Does he have some sort of lie detector that I don't know about?

"Hang on," he says and leaves the room, sliding his hand against my arm as he goes.

The door. Of course it's the door. I squeeze my eyes shut. I've made everything that little bit worse, haven't I? If I explain about Danny and how we only have each other, ever since our grandparents died, Hudson will be fine. Right?

He comes back in with a manilla envelope.

"The wicked never rest." I point at the flat package that looks to have documents in it. "Work."

He tosses it down on the desk near the window. "The New York gift and curse, anything delivered by courier any time." Then he frowns. "I'm an ass, Scarlett. I know you're doing this for me, but my mother mentioned a career plan?"

"I panicked. I mean, I'm into studying and developing artificial intelligence, but I'm not even on the bottom rung."

College was great and then our grandparents died and Danny had his career mapped so I decided to help with that while I sorted my own things out and weeks led to months and…well…here I am.

"I'd like to hear about it."

I wave a hand at him. "It's boring."

"You know, I don't think there's anything boring about you, Scarlett. Or anything you do."

My heart twists and I have to tell him the truth. Find a way to make it sweeter than it is, bring it down to what it is, a small lie. A girl who helped him, that's all.

But I do need to say something because he told me he trusts me and wants to see me after all this and…oh, crap, I want that, too.

"Hudson?"

"Yeah?" He smiles at me. And it's the loveliest, most open thing I've seen. The trust almost knocks me over.

And it hits me.

My white lie that spawned all these others, that lie is now not really white and not really small. That's simply me being desperate. He's not going to be understanding if I tell him. He'll put a stop to it. Better to get through this now.

If I keep all that to myself, and keep it contained, maybe buy some extra duct tape for the soul, I can push through and save all this for him. And once that is done, I'll take my chances and come clean.

If he never wants to see me, so be it, but I don't want it to be a situation where he just walks away from his own wants and needs.

I can't let him down.

Telling him the truth will do just that.

Instead, I do the one thing I know I can think of. Slowly, I walk up to him and smile. It's easy to do. The man is gorgeous and hot and sparks ignite when we touch. I stop in front of him and slide my hands up the front of his waistcoat and I toy with the top button.

"I was thinking," I say, popping that button free as his hands come up to my waist and he pulls my shirt free. "That we didn't get to explore the possibilities of this room."

His blue eyes are fire that I want to lose myself in and I do because it's a better place than reality. The other reality. This reality, I'll take. "I see. What did you have in mind?"

"This." And I kiss him.

He kisses me back in a slow, deliberately bone-melting seduction. It's full of low burning embers that could melt iron and I'm only flesh and blood.

His hands are sliding higher as he explores my flesh beneath my shirt and I'm fumbling with the buttons, down and down until it's open, and then I go for the shirt, all the while he whispers caresses against my fevered skin, his mouth open and wet, his teeth the right level of graze, his tongue a tease as he makes little paths over my throat, up to my ear and to my mouth.

I'm lost and all I can do is lose myself deeper in this, and I pull at his clothes, and he pulls at mine until there's enough there to make this work.

Hudson only breaks the kisses to slide another piece of my clothes off and I'm stroking over the hot, hard flesh on his chest, moving down to his cock and undoing the fly and then he picks me up and I'm naked. How did he do that with such deftness?

And then I stop thinking as he deposits me on the desk, pulling me forward until I'm spread open before him.

"Beautiful," he says, his gaze moving over me, and then he traces a line from my right nipple to the left and then down over my quivering stomach until he reaches my pussy and he teases with merciless light touches until he grabs his cock in his hand and lines it up.

My gasp of delight is audible as he pushes slowly into me, inch by inch, until he's stretched me out and buried to the hilt.

"Scarlett..." And he takes my mouth as I wrap my arms and legs about him and we set up a slow, scandalous rhythm, not hard and fast and wild, but just as breathtaking. Maybe more so, because there's something else here in our coming together. A deeper, sweeter, more real connection, and we move together, each of us elevating the other until we have something new, something so mind-blowingly gorgeous I come, my orgasm a deep, bone shaking rolling wave of intense pleasure that won't stop. And I dig my short nails into him and whisper his name in a moan as I keep coming, and then he comes too, and we both keep going until there's nothing left.

Just him.

And me.

Together.

Chapter Twenty-Seven

HUDSON

The house seems emptier now she's gone.

After the sex that took me to a completely new level I didn't know existed, a level I don't know what to do with because it doesn't fit with my life and beliefs, Scarlett got a text. Her roommate, I think. I wasn't paying that close attention because as we dressed I needed to get myself together.

So I let her go. I'll see her in the morning at work.

I've worked out, showered and now I'm back in the room that smells like the best sex I've ever had.

The envelope is on the floor and I pick it up, tapping it against my other hand.

I'd almost forgotten about this.

So much has happened since I asked for the information I ordered after I found out about the meeting. I'm not an idiot and I don't let things just sit when I can get a jump start.

Work smart, not just hard. That's the rule.

The private investigator sent the info package by courier. I didn't put a rush order on it, just said I needed it a week before the date I provided.

Information on the lovely Scarlett. That's what's in here.

It's not that I don't trust her. I do. It's that with this information I can study up and not ask her boring questions. I just wanted a cheat deep dive into knowing her, the stuff we've been over and the stuff I might find useful in the meeting.

To make it fair, I had the same information on me sent to her, so when she gets to the office in the morning, it'll be there, waiting for her. This way we can go in completely prepared.

I throw myself onto the sofa and run my thumb along the seal, opening it.

Pulling it out I start to read.

And everything goes cold.

I'm the world's biggest moron. I have to be. I've been blindsided by pretty.

Fucking Scarlett. She's done the one thing I can't stand. The one thing I won't stand.

Scarlett lied to me.

I'm in the office early, even for me. And I know I look like shit.

That's not surprising as I couldn't sleep.

I picked up the phone about ten times to call her. And put it down each and every time.

I thought about calling Kingston or Magnus. Ryder was out of the question, because he'd just say fuck her, use her, move on. To be fair, they all would, but that would be the beginning and end of his advice. And with the others…there's nothing they could say I haven't thought myself.

My door is firmly shut with strict orders not to be disturbed left via text with my receptionist as soon as I got here.

Except, that is, Scarlett.

The fucking liar.

I don't have long to wait when the work day starts. After a crisp knock, Scarlett breezes in, smiling and happy and I take her in, my blood ice in my veins, anger beating in my heart.

She looks like that flower field, fresh and bright like the sun's just kissed the morning dew. How she worked out to play me for money is anyone's guess. She's not my type. Yet she worked some kind of dark magic on me, anyway.

She's wearing a very pretty dress, all flowy in the right places, the tiny cream dots on the black material fetching against her dark honey hair. And beneath her arm is that manilla folder I forgot to take from her desk.

"Scarlett."

She starts to bound over to me but she sees something in my face and stops, a small frown forming as the morning sun decides to struggle out from the blanket gray sky and adorn her just like she's in that stupid field I made up.

I really am the worst kind of moron.

"Hudson? Is something wrong?"

"You tell me." I fold my hands in front of me on my desk and keep my best poker face on.

"Well—"

"I'll help you out, Scarlett. You lied."

She goes pale. Not even the hint of dew about her now, but I bet she smells just as good as always.

I wait for her to say something, anything, but she doesn't. She's seemingly stuck to the spot, unable to move or speak, so I help her out.

"You lied to me. I don't know how you got away with it or why you did it..." I rake my gaze over her. "Money, I'm guessing."

"Hudson—"

"But that doesn't matter. You lied and that's why this whole thing won't work. We'll never get through this."

"We can, I know it. I'm sorry, I should have said something earlier. But I do know Sarah."

"Oh, I know. It's in the report I got on you. I had you investigated, Scarlett."

The look of horror makes me laugh and I'm feeling mean.

"What? You thought I wouldn't do that? I told you there's a lot riding on this, and I told you I expected the best and I expected honesty. The only thing I screwed up was trusting you and not fast tracking the investigation."

She walks right up to the desk. "It's not what you think—"

"Oh, so you're not..." I pull the papers to me, and flip to the page I'm looking for. "From a poor, struggling family where your deadbeat parents took everything and left, and your grandparents ended up bringing you up on what? Hope and a handout?"

She recoils, like I slapped her. "You're upset. I know that. And I should have told you, but just because we didn't have money doesn't mean I can't do this."

"Yes, it does." Cruel. That's what I'm being, I know it and I can't stop because she betrayed me. "No one that knows me would in their right mind think I'd go for you. That I'd choose someone like you."

She nods. "You don't have to be nasty."

"No, I don't, but it's better than what I want to do."

"Which is?"

I stare at her. "I just can't believe you lied and I believed you. Jesus Christ, it's even obvious why you did all this. Your so-called boyfriend?"

"I never said Danny was that."

"No, but you led me to think that. No wonder he looked familiar. Now I know, it's the family resemblance. But even better, I really know who he is now. He's that little shit who practices dodgy real estate and has been trying to get a foot in my door. Which, by the way, will never happen. And I'll make sure he fails on every count anywhere he steps in the tri-state area. He can stay with the bottom feeders."

"You can't do that."

I smile, it's vicious and it's aimed right at her. "I can."

"Please don't take it out on Danny. Please don't." She looks like she's going to cry. "He's decent and he's good at what he does, he's had bad luck and made poor choices in who he trusted—"

"I'll say, if it's you."

She breathes out and half reaches for me and she drops the envelope but makes no move to pick it up as she pulls her hands back in, realizing, it seems, what a futile move she's trying to make. "You don't need to be cruel, Hudson. I screwed up."

"You tried to trick me and you did well, I'll give you that. Better than most. Then again, most don't have the kind of wares you have."

She flinches at the meaning of my words.

"But try and tell me this isn't some sort of scam dreamed up with you and your brother. It was the name, you see, that I put it together. It's in my report who he is, but no photo, as I didn't think I needed that. You tried to use me and you failed."

"Hudson," she says, real panic lighting her voice, "that wasn't my intention. I needed money, but I didn't set out to scam you or trick you or anything. It was one small lie that got out of hand. I'll fix this. All of it."

I've had enough. I stood. "No."

"But we're close—you're close. And everything you said last night, you can't give up now. You don't have to ever see me again after, but we need to see it through."

It's exactly the wrong thing to say to me. I don't need to be reminded of making a fool of myself, of baring parts of my soul to her. I don't need a fucking thing from her except for her to be gone from my life.

"When you leave my office," I say, looking at my watch, "right around now, get your things and go. You're fired. From both jobs. That includes my life, in case I'm not being clear."

"But—"

"Do not make me call security."

Scarlett hesitates and I think she's going to stay, but she doesn't. She nods tightly and turns and leaves, head down.

I sink down into my chair and close my eyes. A weird emptiness spreads through me, somehow weighing me down.

It's over.

And for the first real time in my life, I've failed.

In all the ways that matter.

Chapter Twenty-Eight

SCARLETT

I didn't think it could hurt so much.

But it does.

Even my toes hurt.

Everything that could go wrong, did. I lay on my bed, hugging Mr. Figglesmort to me and close my eyes. When I got home yesterday, I took all the money paid for my work and paid my bills and sent the rest to my brother.

He's been calling, of course he has, but I haven't listened to any messages or read the texts. He needs the money. This is why I did this. I know it's not anything near the amount he needs to dig himself out of the hole and start again, but it's something. I failed.

As for me?

I applied for jobs. After all, what did Hudson say? I'm poor and no one would ever believe he'd choose me. The words, the sentiment sting. I'm not good enough for him. Lower than low.

Worst thing is, I never meant to hurt him at all. I wanted to help. I started out trying to help my brother first and foremost, but even before I got to know Hudson, I'd never have tried to screw him over. Just help. The deeper I got, the more I wanted that.

And now here I am. On my bed at eleven am, hugging a ratty old bear like I'm six. Feeling pathetic and sorry for myself.

The knock on my door rouses me.

With a sigh, I open my eyes, put the bear down and get up, crossing to the door.

Amber's there, a worried expression in her dark eyes. "Should I ask?"

"No."

"He's just a man. And this is New York."

I stop her, putting my hand on her arm. "It's complicated."

"And you're miserable." She gives me a hug, enveloping me in a cloud of spice-laden perfume. "Listen, if this guy doesn't appreciate what he has, then don't fuck him."

And I laugh, in spite of the misery rocking me.

From behind me my phone buzzes and I know it's Danny.

"Scarlett, if you need to get away, say the word. My cousin's got a place upstate, Catskills, it's pretty basic, but it's great and there for the using if you want to just escape...you know..."

"Thanks, Amber. I'll keep it in mind." I give her a hug back. "You're the best."

She winks. "I know! I have to head to work, but just remember, no man is worth misery."

And she's gone. I go to my room and close the door, leaning against it. She might be right, but how do I tell my heart that? I straighten up and go to the bedside table and pick up my phone. Yep, Danny. And this time, I can't miss the text that followed his call.

What the FUCK? Five pm. Essex Wine Bar. NO EXCUSES.

Shit. I do not want to face him and let him down. I'm letting down everyone. The money I sent him isn't going to save him, just buy time and that hurts, too.

I take a breath as I note the time. Thing is, I'm going to have to meet up with him. He's my brother, but I have time to kill today. It's still fairly early, and...

Devastation might have set up house inside me, but I'm not going to let down the other man I love. I can't do anything for Danny—any more than I've done, but I'll be there for him. But Hudson...

I'm not going to let him lose the things that are important to him. I can't.

That's just too much loss and I didn't set out to hurt anyone. He might not want me, but it doesn't matter. Love isn't about gratification, it's about being there and giving, and being the best you can be. I'm not saying hang around when it's futile, but I built this, I also brought it tumbling down. The least I can do is rebuild. For him. And then quietly go away.

I go to grab the manilla envelope and it's not there.

I never opened the thing, but it's got all the information I need in there, and—

Horror spreads through me.

I dropped it. On the floor of his office.

I take a breath and grab my laptop from the bedside table where my phone had been resting and open it up.

All I need is a phone number. Just one. And some luck.

I'm wearing one of the work outfits Amber and I put together as I sit in the quiet, eucalyptus-scented waiting room.

It's cool. Voices are low and it's what I'd expect from a high-end, old school law firm. Stately, traditional, and deceptively lush. Nothing is over the top. Everything costs a fortune, and it does nothing to offend or entice. It just is.

And I'm so nervous that the tiniest sound makes me jump. Like when the receptionist comes up to me and I scream. Just a little.

The elegant woman stares a moment, then smiles politely. "This way."

I'm led down the hushed, wide hall to an office and guided inside. It's just as lovely as the rest, but clearly this isn't an office someone calls home.

After five minutes, I'm about at the end of my tether when someone speaks behind me. "Miss Colton?"

I twist to face him. He's the infamous Jenson, has to be, because this is too important to leave to anyone else. "Yes."

"I'm Edward Jenson, and this is a week early." His gaze is cool as it runs over me and I get the feeling behind that poker face he's surprised by what he sees. I almost say join the club, but somehow, I manage to keep a lid on my mouthiness. "Unusual."

"These are unusual times," I say, aiming for poise and sophistication and missing.

He doesn't move from where he stands. "Usually, I'd have your fiancé here." And his gaze now drops to my hand.

"It's early days. Hudson said this was important to him, and so it's important to me."

"We did have an appointment."

"I know," I say quietly. "Unusual times. Can we...can we start?"

"Do you love him?"

"Yes."

The word is the easiest thing to say and the most painful because I know the love is one sided. Even if we were to make things work out after this, it would always be like that. Because Hudson doesn't believe in love. And that breaks my heart.

"And is he in love with you?"

"He's Hudson." As if that settles the matter. And I clench my hands together and I struggle to stay calm. "But he has his own way, you know? And I'm here."

The man nods slowly. "So you are. Shall we get started?"

The aftermath is a blur. I've no idea how I did, as the questions weren't anything like I thought. Jenson asked if I needed a car anywhere, but I just said I'm heading to the Lower East Side, so I could get there on my own.

I walk, as I have time, and from midtown it's a decent walk through the changing neighborhoods.

I have no idea if what I told him was right, it all felt right. I know enough about Hudson from working with him and spending time with him. And...I did my best. I don't know shoe size or his tailor, but as I said I know Hudson is about quality, not what's labeled the best. That he's the hardest working man I've ever known; and the smooth and sophisticated surface hides so many depths that it would take a lifetime to explore them all.

I cross Essex to the bar, and I'm a few minutes early, but my brother is already there, outside, pacing, waiting for me. He crosses his arms and glares.

"Why did you lie to me?"

"Danny..."

He shook his head. "I warned you about the Sinclair empire, and you went and got involved with Hudson and tried to say you're not?"

"It wasn't like that. I took on a job for him to try and help you, only I—"

"What?"

I swallow, hating that I hurt him. The noise of the street fades to the in my ears as I quickly outline my plan and what happened. Only I don't mention the contract. I don't mention that part at all.

"I knew it," he says when I'm done.

"Knew what?"

"Knew you'd get yourself hurt by working for him. I could sense there was more than you working for Hudson." He sighs. "He isn't for us. I thought I wanted to work for him, but that's out of the picture and nothing will change that."

"You need the money."

Danny nods and slides his hands in his pockets. "You're my big sister and you've taken it on yourself to help me. And that's on me because when I first got in deep shit with my stupid decisions in trusting my business partner I borrowed some money from you. And I've used you as my sounding board and you... Scarlett, you can't fix things for me. I'm not asking and I should never have asked you in the first place. I've had my head up my own ass so long I missed all the signs."

"What signs?" We're outside the bar, but right now, I wish we were inside, and I was knee deep in drinks. But something tells me drowning my sorrows isn't going to help.

He toes a piece of old newspaper on the pavement with his boot. "Everything you've been doing since college. You had plans, Scarlett, until you didn't. At first, I figured the years of odd jobs were a way to save up to go to grad school. But there's been a letter buried on your coffee table from Berkley."

I stare at him. "There is?" Then I bite my lip. "I forgot about that. I didn't open it. I need to throw that out."

"It was an offer of a place way back at the beginning of the year. I know, I opened it. I only just started thinking about it with all this. And the huge amount of money you sent me."

"I can't afford that degree. It's not a scholarship."

"You could if you used this money."

"It's yours."

He sighs and steps up to me and gives me a hug, and I stay there, listening to the steady, familiar beat of my brother's heart. "I'm not a kid. And I'd rather you respected that, Scarlett." He kisses the top of my head. "These are my mistakes and I'll find a way to fix them, and make my career happen—even if I have to abandon it for now while I get out there and work. I'm not taking your money, okay?"

"I did it for you." I try to pull free, but my brother tightens his hold.

"Yeah, and we're okay, honestly. I love you and I'm going to be better than okay, but you have to look after you, not me."

This time I pull away. "Danny, I always keep my eye out on you. I promised Gran—"

"But you took on more than you should, more than I wanted you to do. Now, I've got a meeting here at the bar for a job. I'm thinking I can work here, and start from scratch with the real estate, you know? Rebrand, start renting out little places here and there and build. But first, I'm going to earn the money, not you. And if you like this Hudson—"

"Don't." I wrap my arms around my waist. "I screwed that up, too. And—"

"You've a good heart, Scarlett. I don't know all the details, only you took on a job with him, but…" He smiles like he suspects there's more to it than I've told him. "If he doesn't see what he's got, then he doesn't deserve you. Because maybe you took the job to help me, get in with him, put in a good word, but you care about him."

"Go to your interview. We'll talk tomorrow."

"We're good?"

"We are."

I sniff and my eyes get a little blurry as he goes into the bar. I'm sort of at a loss on the street. All I've done is just make a huge mess of everything. Even Danny claims he doesn't need my help and I did all that for…what?

I guess it doesn't matter. I'm on my own, needing a job. And maybe I can go back to my AI work. Maybe a move would be good. I don't know. I start towards the train when a sleek, spotless cream-colored car pulls to a stop and a door opens.

It's Faye. Hudson's mother. She's looking completely perfect as usual and she pats the seat next to her. "Get in. Please."

I'm so shocked I do.

"Scarlett. I was waiting for you."

I frown. "How did... Did you follow me?"

His mother smiles.

It's the only explanation I can think of. Either that or she's got some scary ass psychic powers.

"I've been talking to Jenson. But I have to say, you did a good job. Had me fooled."

"Excuse me?"

"The falling in love thing with my son. He put you up to this, didn't he? How much did he pay you?"

Everything in me is white cold. The one thing I thought maybe I got right—helping Hudson get what he wanted—I clearly failed. "What are you talking about?"

"You're not from the Meriweather family, and my son doesn't believe in love."

Shit. "That's something you have to ask him. About the love, anyway. But don't blame him. Don't punish him. I only ever lied to him about my background and that was wrong, but...I did it to win him, to get him to see me." Great, now I'm making him sound like the worst kind of snob. "But Hudson...he's difficult and sometimes I want to scream, but I love him. I fell in love with him, and I lied to get the job, used my friend's background and then...we got to know each other."

She's just looking at me, not saying a word and I'm...not lying...only omitting the contractual part of it because as I say this, it's true. I did lie to get a job, and then we got to know each other, and then...

"I don't know if Hudson will forgive me for my small lie to get the job. But everything else...him and me...it's true, and he doesn't deserve to lose out on family history, on something that means the world to him, because I screwed it up."

"Scarlett?"

"Yes?"

She smiles, and it's sweet and genuine, and my eyes blur all over again. Damn these stupid tears, anyway. "Have you told my son that?"

"No. He's mad at me."

"Maybe you should. While there's time."

She taps the glass and we take off and I'm too caught up in the wild ride of emotions inside to even question where we're going until we stop.

I look out the window.

Hudson's home.

"I..."

"I hope to see you again, Scarlett," she says, with a nod to the door.

My fingers are ice as I open it, and as her car zooms away, I slowly turn and look at Hudson's place.

At the very least, I need to tell him about what I did today.

I do think he's worth it. And I now have to go do the hardest thing of all.

Face Hudson.

Chapter Twenty-Nine

HUDSON

The flames in my little-used fireplace in the drawing room I also barely use eat the paper.

I stare, getting nothing, not even grim satisfaction at watching the fucking unopened dossier on myself and the NDA and contract burn.

Scarlett hadn't even bothered opening it. That's how much of a terrible scam artist she is. Or is that good?

I'm not really sure because she got me good. Tied me in knots and had me believing—well that doesn't matter.

Or maybe not opening it was a big screw you to me.

Who knows?

I worked from home today because after she left yesterday, I didn't think another day of me like that inflicted on my staff would be good for morale. The unemployment line, perhaps, but not morale.

Standing, I go over to the tightly shut window and think about letting in the light of day or what's left of it, but I don't see the point in that either. There's something big and dark and restless in me. And it weighs me down. It's also got claws and it feels like I'm bleeding inside.

My phone rings for about the hundredth time that day and I ignore it. The last few were Jenson. I don't want to speak to him. Or my brothers. And certainly not my mother.

Scarlett has taken my advice and kept away, and I tell myself I'm glad.

When it rings again, I stalk over to it and pick it up. I could smash it to pieces, but the short-lived satisfaction isn't enough for the headache that will bring. And...it's Jenson. Again.

"What?"

"Charm like that and you'll be mistaken for your father," he says in smooth tones.

"I'm not in the mood. I left word the meeting's canceled. It's all canceled. You win. My father wins."

He pauses a moment, and I can hear the leather of his chair as he shifts. "It's not a competition."

"Yeah?" I rub a spot on my chest that both feels heavy and empty and aching all at once. I know I should try and get what's mine here. I'm built for this. To win against the odds, to find the way in and trick the system. Smart over hard work, that's the rule. And do whatever it takes.

I should, but I ease down on the settee I think I might hate. I've never thought about this room much. It serves its purpose with certain guests. But right now, it feels like I'm in some bespoke hotel and nothing seems to fit.

"So, by your message and...this I take it you're just giving up?"

"Why would you care?" I'm taking it out on Jenson and I'm trying to feel guilty, but when I look at it, everything comes back to him. If he'd quietly lost that fucking letter, I wouldn't have met Scarlett and I wouldn't be feeling like this. Lost and broken.

I'm just not sure why.

I like her. I'm into her—or was. I find her hot and insanely fuckable. But hormones and attraction are reactions, not anything more.

"Because it's my job." For a man who keeps it bland and calming there's a lot of sarcasm in that answer but I let it slide.

"Fine. Yes, I'm giving up. I made a mistake. Happy?" I don't give him time to answer. "I was a fool and I fell for someone who only wanted money."

Those words were an attempt to perhaps pave another path in, but as I say them there's something to them, something I don't want to go near at all.

I could have almost any damn woman I want. They practically throw themselves at me and my brothers, so why her?

"There's no other way, Hudson. Say the word and I'll meet up and we'll have that interview. Maybe you and your girl can work it out."

"She's not my anything. Not anymore," I say. "So what's the point? I lost."

And I disconnect the call.

My words ring in my head. Loud.

I lost. In more devastating ways than a trinket. More than family history. That last one shocks me. Family and tradition and the history and sanctity of the Sinclair clan is important to me, but all I can see is Scarlett and that dark honeyed hair.

I'm hurting and I'm furious because she's not what I thought she was, not what I was discovering and continuing to discover. All I'd found was a pretty bundle of lies.

The door rings and I rise and stalk out of the room and down the hall and pull it open.

I can't breathe.

Scarlett.

Pale and scared and breaking my heart with those big hazel eyes. Breaking my heart, if I had one that believed in love.

"I thought we should talk," she said, moving from one foot to the other as if she's half thinking of running away. "I already spoke to your lawyer."

"Oh, you did? Trying to get a sweeter cut of the fucking pie?" Her words are a red flag to my raging bull and the fury takes over. I want to lash out, but all I can do is push her away. "I'll give you whatever you want. I've destroyed the NDA and the contract, you're free to do whatever you damn like, and I'll pay you the money. Just go and do whatever it is far away from me."

And I don't give her a chance to respond. I just walk in and slam the door.

It should feel better than it does.

But it doesn't.

It feels like utter hell.

I'm three drinks into the bottle of whiskey and I'm not planning on stopping any time soon. My anger is still at nuclear levels but there's something else there, as I toy with the glass, staring into the contents, that I don't like.

Regret? Self-doubt? I don't know and I don't care. Magnus has called me a few times, and my mother. But I ignore them all. Just like before.

I slammed the door on Scarlett about an hour ago and even I have to admit it was a low moment. Low and pathetic and not something I do.

Cool and calm and smoothly calculating, that's me. The man who works hard and only has time to play on his tightly controlled schedule. Fits of passion aren't me unless they're in the bedroom and...

Even then, it's getting off for me and the lady in question. On finding the release. But Scarlett got down in deep and it became a clawing need I couldn't control.

I shove my hand through my hair and consider throwing the handmade antique glass.

Actually consider it.

For the second time that evening, I'm thinking about destroying something. Something shifted inside and I can't get it to move back. It's like Scarlett invaded and decimated and—

The doorbell rings.

"For fuck's sake." I slam the glass down on the delicate side table next to the settee, and I don't know why I'm back in this room, maybe it's because it's the least like me and therefore doesn't seem infused with her, even though she hasn't been in most of my place, I slam it down and stalk to the door, ripping it open.

"Mr. Sinclair, I'm—"

"Scarlett's brother. I don't want to see her and I don't want to see you," I snarl at the light brown haired man who, now I know who he is, I see the resemblance. "You can go."

I start to turn, but his hand comes up and catches the door. I look at it and then at him, but Danny doesn't release the door and I do have a spark of respect for that. A small one.

After all, no doubt he was in on the whole fucking thing.

"No."

"Excuse me?" I say.

"I said no." Danny's shaking a little, but he lifts his chin and looks me in the eye. I have staff who've worked for me for years who wouldn't do that when faced with me in this mood. "You know, for years, ever since I got into real estate—and no, you don't know me, I'm the smallest of the bottom feeders, and I'm honest—I saw your empire as my dream. I wanted to be good enough to work for you."

"They all want to be agents who deal with the best clients and rake in the big bucks. I've heard it before."

Danny smiles a little. "I wanted to work with the best of the best. Small can be good, too, and not every client will rake it in, but I guess you wouldn't know that. Too big. Too heartless. See, I made one mistake. I trusted my partner a little too much when I set out and he stole everything and blackened my name."

"If you're here to beg for a job, I don't hire the Colton family."

The smile vanishes. "No. I wouldn't work for a man like you. How you treated Scarlett? Never. She's worth a million of you."

"She lied to me. Tried to scam me."

"Scarlett?" Danny laughs and shakes his head. "Never in a million years. She didn't tell you she wasn't rich and then she fell for you, and she tried to help me. And even though you stomped over her, she tried to help you."

"What are you on about?" I have a whiskey with my name on it and this kid is annoying the shit out of me. Or maybe he's making me uncomfortable when he speaks of Scarlett, hitting a little too close to the marrow.

He glares at me. "The only thing Scarlett's ever been guilty of—apart from opening her mouth before thinking some things through—is having a giant heart. You don't deserve her and I'd rather clean toilets than work for you."

"Why are you here?"

"To tell you that you're a class A idiot."

And with that, he lets go of the door and walks off.

After he's gone, I look at my whiskey in the drawing room but I don't want it anymore. Danny Colton's words haunt me. I am an idiot. And what's worse, is he'd be the kind of person I'm interested in hiring.

Or investing in, if he's to be believed in the little people comment. I have small businesses I support, ones who don't fit in with me, but I invest in and regardless of what he said, I make a note on my phone to have him looked into—properly. He was courageous and determined and he stood up to me.

If he's got what I like, I'll take him on, or invest, or both. My business is something I know. And regardless of what I said about not ever hiring him, I will if he's what I want.

But the rest of it? Scarlett? That's done and dusted.

Problem is, it doesn't feel like that. And her brother's words haunt me as I haunt my home for the next hour. I can't sit. I can't work. I'm not interested in eating. And even the booze lost its charm.

I want something, but I don't know what it is.

Suddenly, I stop and close my eyes.

Yes, I do.

I want Scarlett.

I don't stop to think as I call for my car. The ride to Brooklyn seems to take forever, but finally we're there. I hit the ground at a run and ring her doorbell.

We can talk. We can—

"What are you doing here?"

It's her roommate, dressed up and heading out the front door of the building. My finger is still on the buzzer.

"I'm here to see Scarlett."

"She's not here, asshole. She's gone."

I frown. "What do you mean, gone?"

The girl gets in my face. "Like gone in a puff of smoke and not coming back. See ya. Wouldn't want to be ya."

She saunters off over the cracked pavement, high fiving a guy who's pants ride low under his boxers as she goes.

I pull out my phone to call Scarlett, but it's straight to voicemail.

There's no one else I can speak to. And Scarlett...

I fucked the hell up.

She's gone.

That rocks me right down into the ground and I can't breathe. It's like a boot, crushing my ribs into dust.

I get back in the car and we return to Manhattan.

I'm a successful businessman. A billionaire. I can be ruthless. I stop at nothing to get what I want. But I've lost before. In different ways. Deals, businesses, investments. I always thought I understood the meaning of losing.

But I haven't.

Until now.

Because I just realized I've lost the one thing I didn't think I had.

I've gone and lost my heart.

Chapter Thirty

SCARLETT

I never thought of myself as a glutton for punishment. But here I am, hungry, it seems, for more.

Honestly, I should have taken up the offer of the Catskills. I almost did. But I was leaving for a bus to take me, keys are in my bag, when some kid gave me a printed note. Old school, but the paper's expensive and it isn't signed, and the kid said the guy gave him fifty bucks.

So here I am, back at Hudson's place in the East Sixties, the streetlamps casting dappled light through the trees and couples strolling with dogs and cyclists zipping along make it all seem idyllic.

Seem being the word.

The note had to be from Hudson. Who else would send me something that said we need to talk?

I take a breath and force myself on reluctant legs to go to his door.

He doesn't take long to answer this time, and he isn't as ferocious as he was earlier. But he looks disheveled and he's staring at me like I'm some horrible ghost.

No...he's staring at me like he can't believe I'm there. The rest of his expression I can't read, but there's something in his dark blue eyes that causes my heart to lurch and fill with a little hope.

"I got your note," I say in a rush, holding it out.

Hudson takes it and scans it in moments. I mean, it's four words long. Then he looks back at me. "Not mine."

"Oh." I swallow, taking the note and crumpling it in one hand. "It's not a ruse to see you. I promise. You made it very clear—"

"That has my mother all over it, trying to be me."

"Why—" I stop. What am I even doing? He doesn't want me here. "I'll go."

I turn but Hudson speaks, stopping me.

"She thinks she can meddle, apparently. Used to do that when I fought with my brothers. When we were teenagers."

I nod and force myself to take a step.

His voice is soft when he speaks next. And it almost floors me. "Scarlett...don't go."

"Why?"

"Because I thought you'd gone and I think she's right. Come in. Please. Then you can go. After we talk."

That...doesn't sound overly promising, no matter what my heart might be thinking, but even if it's the faintest hope, I have to take it. And I need to tell him how I feel.

So I turn and slip in past him, careful not to touch him and then I stop as he shuts the door, unsure which way to go.

"This way," he says, moving ahead of me and pointing into a room I haven't been in.

Any other time and I'd be fascinated. This is not him. At all. This has the fingerprints of an interior designer who went with tasteful money and didn't know him at all. Hudson has taste, but not delicate pieces of furniture that make a statement.

He likes simplicity in his home if his bedroom is anything to go by. Even in his office...it's beautiful, gorgeous pieces, an antique desk from the look of it, but it's all functional, masculine without hitting anyone on the head, and it's understated. This...is not.

"Who did the room?"

"Someone I hired. I don't use a lot of the place. Why?"

I shrug. "It's not you."

He goes over to a drinks cart that's straight out of a Gatsby wet dream and pours two drinks and hands me one. I hold it because I don't know what else to do with it.

"I came here because...I've gone and fallen in love with you." He doesn't say a word, so I plunge on. "And I never in a million years meant to hurt you or screw up the job you hired me for. That's why I—"

This time I take a sip of the smooth whiskey and I continue. "I never thought my lies would cause this havoc. The reason I mentioned the lawyer is I demanded the interview and I hope to God I did right. I didn't open that package you got for me, the one on you, and that wasn't out of anything other than I didn't get around to it. And the thing is, I already know all the things that matter about you. When I saw it, I thought it was the updated contract you wanted me to sign."

"I see."

I bite my lip. "I know the report you left for me might have contained information, like when you lost your first tooth or the name and address of your first girlfriend, and I know you don't believe in love. I'm not asking for that back. But I didn't need to read the report, Hudson, because that stuff, that's just details. Things anyone can find out. I know you."

He's just standing there, like he's frozen, his expression betraying nothing, his focus completely on me.

So I continue. "You're a martini with complexity. You're a good boss and demanding. You work way too much, but you also love it. And...and you have a good heart, Hudson. Otherwise, you'd have made good on your word to finish me and those I love. You don't speak idly. You have purpose. And you're funny. You might not get my dumb references, but you know how to laugh and make jokes and poke fun at yourself and I've never seen you be mean to anyone, no matter who they are. Okay, me. But I deserved it. And you can dance. You're a little wild in there, just like the perfect martini. Packing all the right punches in the right way."

I set the drink down on the delicate side table and I cross the handwoven soft beige and earth-colored rug to the door to the hall.

Still not a word from Hudson and I nod, my heart shriveling up, all the hope gone. He doesn't need to love me. It's not a selfish thing, me loving him. It just is. And I've said my piece. Except one thing.

"You're a good man. And I think you believe in love, deep down. Not with me. But I hope you find the right person."

"Do you?"

I nod again, pressing my lips together, wanting desperately not to cry here. But I'm so close. "I need to go. I thought all of this, what we set out to do, would be easy."

"Yeah," he says, putting his drink on the trolley. "I thought so, too."

"Goodbye, Hudson."

"You know what?" He doesn't wait for me to answer. He keeps speaking. "Fuck it."

"Excuse me?"

"I said fuck it. Fuck the damn Sinclair jewel. Fuck my wounded pride, fuck everything. It's not worth it."

"What are you saying?" My head is starting to spin and I grab hold of the doorway.

Hudson starts crossing to me in slow, measured steps. "I'm saying I worked something out tonight. I do believe in love. If it's you. I'm in love with you, too. And, Scarlett, nothing is worth losing you. Not my stupid pride, not a jewel, not even my piece of the family business and my heritage. Because without you, that's just meaningless shit."

He's in front of me now, so close and the sweet tension that exists between us rises, made sweeter by the singing in my blood and the sudden lightness in my heart. He traces the curve of my cheek with his finger and I sigh, a tear slipping free. One he catches and smooths away with his thumb.

"I want you, Scarlett. You. Your mouthiness and inappropriate comments. The way you think and move and challenge me. I've never felt like this before and I'm going to make mistakes. Hopefully not like this one, but I know I will. I'm not infallible. And I need you, too. Since you came and worked for me, life got more interesting, it got better. And I'm always going to be Hudson Sinclair, so I have to say that my work life got better. You have a way of doing things in all walks of life that I need. I'm not good at going outside the box in the way you are. And you don't have to work for me, but if you could help me train your replacement and then you can do whatever you damn well want. I'm going to need you."

"You are?"

Hudson smiles slowly. "You're going to be involved in developing those damn AIs that are going to take over the planet, so I'd like to be by your side."

I suddenly laugh. "You're admitting you're using me as your personal shield?"

"I don't lie." His smile fades. "Joking aside, I'm ridiculously in love with you. I never realized it until I thought I'd lost you. Marry me, Scarlett."

"Yes."

It's that easy to say, that word to his question. I'm spinning and I don't care. I throw my arms around him and go to kiss him when his doorbell rings.

Hudson groans. "I'm having that removed. Wait here."

I do. I even do a little dance while he's gone. Maybe this is fast, but I don't care. I want to be with him. I've never felt like this before and it feels utterly right. Like something clicked into place.

"Scarlett?"

I go still. He has a manilla padded envelope in one hand that's open, and he holds something in the other. He shows me. On a piece of paper with writing is a ring. It's utterly beautiful. A pink diamond.

"Is that...?"

"Yeah. My Sinclair jewel." He drops the envelope and takes my hand. "And a note. I passed, apparently."

I try to read the cursive script upside down but can't. "That's a lot of words for that."

"It says to keep the family business that means something beyond money to the Sinclair brothers, each and every one of them will be given their own test, with four weeks, within a twelve-month period. If they don't pass, they lose the Sinclair family business. Out of private and into public hands. It will be lost forever."

I gasp. "But—"

"I'll let my brothers know tomorrow," he says, dropping the note and pulling me closer. He still has the ring in his hand, though. "But this is their problem now, not mine."

"Hudson. We're talking the family legacy, something that's beyond important to you."

"All my life, that was right, but not anymore. Don't get me wrong, I want to keep it in the family, but you mean more to me."

I'm trying to breathe, my heart almost bursting. "What do you mean?"

"I mean, my sweet Scarlett—" he slips the ring on my finger "—is I have something better to live for. You."

"Stop it. You'll make me cry." I look at the ring, and it's beautiful, almost as beautiful as him. It's slightly loose, but I don't care. I meet his gaze as I slide my hands up around his neck.

He kisses me, soft and loving and full of hope and the future. And then he says, against my mouth, "We can start our own legacy. One built from love. What do you say?"

"Yes."

And when we kiss, it's the beginning of our own legacy. This is no dark inheritance. It's new. A bright, shining future full of love.

This is the end of Hudson and Scarlett's love story.
But the two, as well as all the other Sinclair brothers, return, very soon
Would you like to browse through my other books and read another of my romance novels?
Click here:
https://mybook.to/hLSVaJ

***

Or would you like to read my free enemies-to-lovers-romance "Date with Hate"?
Then, click here and subscribe and get your free copy instantly into your inbox:
https://sendfox.com/rebeccabaker

Afterword

Dear reader,

I really hope you enjoyed this story. If so, I would appreciate a short review on Amazon. As an indie author, I don't have the resources of a major publisher, so this is the way you would support me the most.

***

A little note at the end

You will look for contraceptives in vain in this book. Why is that? The story takes place in your imagination and should give you a carefree time and carefree reading pleasure.

In this world, all billionaires have six-packs and are really good in bed. STDs don't exist in this world.

My free romance novel

Eould you like to read my free enemies-to-lovers-romance "Date with Hate"? Then, click here and subscribe and get your free copy instantly into your inbox:
https://sendfox.com/rebeccabaker

Printed in Great Britain
by Amazon